Men of Wisdom

GEORGE FOX
AND THE QUAKERS

by

HENRY VAN ETTEN

Translated and Revised

by

E. KELVIN OSBORN

NEW YORK	LONDON
HARPER TORCHBOOKS	LONGMANS

ENGLISH TRANSLATION © LONGMANS, GREEN & CO LTD 1959

The Quakers' Meeting, by Egbert Hemskerck, the Younger, who came to England
from Holland in 1689. There are several versions of this caricature; a French
version is shown on p. 130; their common feature is the woman on the tub; she may
be translating into Dutch for George Fox.

CONTENTS

Four rulers of England in the 16th century.

The English Revolution and
the Origins of the Society of Friends

It was in the spring of 1652 that George Fox, a powerfully built, youngish-looking man of twenty-eight, reached Lancashire in the course of his wanderings. Fired with zeal like a Hebrew prophet, he had fought his way through years of lonely searching for Truth, and had by now gathered friends about him.

> As we went [he said, echoing the poetry of the Book of Revelation] I spied a great high hill called Pendle Hill, and I went on the top of it with much ado, it was so steep; but I was moved of the Lord to go atop of it; and when I came atop of it I saw Lancashire sea; and there atop of the hill I was moved to sound the day of the Lord; and the Lord let me see atop of the hill in what places he had a great people to be gathered. As I went down, on the hill side I found a spring of water and refreshed myself, for I had eaten little and drunk little for several days.
>
> And so at night we came to an alehouse. . . . And the Lord opened to me at that place, and let me see a great people in white raiment by a river's side coming to the Lord, and the place was near John Blaykling's where Richard Robinson lived.
>
> And the next day we passed on . . . and at night we got a little ferns or brackens and lay upon a common . . . (pp. 103–4).[1]

This vision of great numbers of people in the Lune valley up to Sedbergh was to be fulfilled within a few weeks in that spring of 1652, and in the course of the next few years the followers of George Fox came to be numbered in tens of thousands; it is rightly regarded as the beginning of the religious movement called the Society of Friends or Quakers. Let us briefly consider the political and religious situation which brought it into being.

[1] The page numbers appended to extracts from Fox's *Journal* relate to the full text edited by John Nickalls (Cambridge University Press, 1952), unless otherwise stated.

In the lifetime of these four men, George Fox grew up and established his movement.

The English Revolution of the mid-seventeenth century, culminating in the great achievements of religious toleration and constitutional monarchy, was a product of many forces; the deepest and most powerful of these was religion—a personal religion, notably among the common people, based on a study of the Bible and of the many works of devotion that poured from the presses in the sixty years up to 1640. For example, Arthur Dent's *A Plaine Man's Pathway to Heaven* went through twenty-five editions between 1601 and 1640.

The first complete English translation of the Bible, initiated by John Wycliffe and completed before his death in 1384, was banned. In the following century Tyndale, the contemporary of the Reformers Luther and Calvin, had to leave England in order to produce his translation of the Bible. 'If God spare my life,' he once said to an acquaintance, 'ere many years I will cause a boy that driveth the plough shall know more of the Scripture than thou dost.' The importation of his New Testament was ineffectively forbidden in 1526. After Henry VIII had cut off the Church in England from the Pope's authority for reasons that were far from religious, an official English version of the Bible was placed in parish churches, and the Bible began to permeate the life of the country as a whole. The newness and wonder of the book, for its hearers in that generation, can still be sensed by anyone who opens one of those old copies and reads the excited introduction: a new world of thought and emotion was being revealed to the English people.

The Protestant Reformation, substituting the stern authority of the Bible for that of the Pope, made headway in parts of continental Europe, and held brief sway in England in the reign of the boy-king Edward VI (1547–53): it was then that the great English prayer-book was drawn up. His successor Mary restored Catholicism for five years, but disgusted the country by burning 300 obstinate Protestants in her last three years. The accession of Elizabeth I brought the firm enforcement of a compromise form of worship, called Anglicanism, which has survived as the State religion of England. The Queen was the head of the Church; services were in English; but the ritual

The Anabaptist. The Brownist.

The Familia. The Papist.

all Independants

Four groups fighting for the Bible, (1641). Brownists are now Congregationalists, and the Familists died out.

resembled that of the Church of Rome. During her forty-five years' reign, and partly owing to Spanish attempts to recruit a fifth column among English Catholics, religious persecution fell with increasing severity on those who would not conform to the religious code, both on Puritans who wished to purify the Church from Romish practices, but remained within the Church of England, and also on the Catholics who stood outside it.

James I, who succeeded to the throne in 1603, authorized a new translation of the Bible. This brilliant version, produced by a commission of translators at the moment when the language of England was at its most beautiful, was largely based on Tyndale's, and for 300 years remained the chief background to English thought and imagery. The Puritans were soon disappointed in their hope of receiving more liberty of conscience from James who, as a Scottish Presbyterian, might have been expected not to enforce uniformity according to the Church of England. But he did so; and increasing numbers of those who took religion seriously emigrated across the Atlantic. The Pilgrim Fathers are only the best-known of them.

In 1625, Charles I came to the throne and, some years later,

William Laud became successively Bishop of London and Archbishop of Canterbury. He was head of the High Church party, fiercely opposed to the Puritan anti-Catholics. Between 1630 and 1639, the king and the archbishop missed no opportunity of persecuting the Puritans; on the other hand the Roman Catholic authorities looked favourably on Laud's activities. In this atmosphere, it was easy for Charles I's French wife, Queen Henrietta Maria, to exercise her influence as head of the Catholic party in England. Although it was very unpopular in the country, Catholicism had become the fashion at Court. The field was left all the freer for a return to Rome, since thousands of Puritans were leaving for America every year.

No heretic had been burned in England since 1612, but in 1639 the Privy Council, encouraged by Archbishop Laud, seriously considered burning a working mason as an example to heretics. The counts on which he was charged cast a sharp light on the growing independence of thought in the working classes: he was accused of non-attendance at church, of studying the Bible at home, of being against printed prayers, and of being opposed to the system of bishops. A hundred years of thoughtful Bible-study and of the sincerity of independent groups of worshippers such as the Familists (members of a sect called the Family of Love) and the Baptists, had helped to bring the English people to the edge of revolt in both religion and politics.

Many sects sprang up in the 1640s. This picture was published in 1644.

Never before or since have they been so stirred by arguing about religious dogmas; this became the chief occupation of men of letters and professors, of merchants at their counters, of labourers at their work, of women busy at home, and even of boys and girls at play. The outbreak of the first Civil War in 1642 put an end to the effective enforcement of religious uniformity; and in this time of unlooked-for liberty of worship sects sprang up among the common people. Their members, a negligible handful before 1640, grew in ten years to such strength that they gained control of the army, executed the king, and founded a Commonwealth.[1]

By 1645 Ephraim Pagit had published a description of these sects in his *Heresiography*, and in 1646 the Presbyterian writer Thomas Edwards described in shocked tones 176 'errors, heresies, blasphemies' in his *Gangroena*. There were the Fifth Monarchy Men, who expected the millennium immediately; there were Ranters, who exalted private judgement above everything else; and 'every counsel of perfection seemed capable of immediate realization'. Yet the conventional forms of religion still afforded a haven for those who were honest and passionately sincere, such as the poet George Herbert, of the High Church party, John Bunyan, who wrote the great epic of Puritanism *The Pilgrim's Progress*, and Richard Baxter the Presbyterian, whose sermons at Kidderminster and elsewhere drew great crowds to hear him.

The first Civil War (1642–6) was won by the Puritans, with the help of the Scots who were interested in setting up Presbyterian Church government in England. The Puritan army had been formed and trained by Cromwell from men of stern moral purpose, and they wanted freedom from the institutional organization of religion. The Presbyterian majority in Parliament, consisting largely of respectable, intolerant men of property, offended the army by trying to suppress all sects other than the Presbyterians; and it was rendered powerless by military defeat in the second Civil War, by Pride's Purge which removed the

[1] See Godfrey Davies, *The Early Stuarts* (Clarendon Press, 1937), p. 192.

George Herbert
(1593–1633).
Poet; author of The
Temple, *one of the*
masterpieces of Eng-
lish poetry.

John Bunyan
(1628–1688).
Baptist mystical writer;
author of The Pilgrim's
Progress.

Richard Baxter
(1615–1691).
Non-conformist theologian
who remained faithful to
the Stuarts though serving
as a Chaplain to the Par-
liament Army.

Presbyterians from the House of Commons, and by the execution of the king (1649). Cromwell was in 1653 forced to govern as a dictator, and until his death in 1658 he maintained religious toleration by the sword. He was not only a military genius, but was great enough to understand and tolerate the blunt sincerity of a man like George Fox. After Cromwell's death, the great, unique army went back to their homes and their farms. The Restoration of Charles II (1660) brought a sharp change: at Whitehall the strict moral code of Cromwell gave place to the excesses of Charles and his mistresses; and in religion the Clarendon Code made final the cleavage between Church and Chapel, Anglicanism and Dissent, Conformity and Non-conformity. Many of the sects died out; but what was worthwhile in Puritanism had struck such deep roots during the Commonwealth that in Charles II's reign, the great persecution—half-hearted by Continental standards, whether of the sixteenth or the twentieth century—failed to stamp it out; and the Act of Toleration of 1689 ensured that men should be relatively free to worship God each in his own way.

The Protestant reformers of the sixteenth century, although just as authoritarian as the Roman Church, left the Bible open for all to ponder. The Protestants believed that revelation had finished, that God had ceased to speak directly within the heart of man. Outside the great Churches, however, there have always been groups of independent mystics, living more or less in concealment and persecution, but who, though unorthodox, hold aloft the burning torch of the Spirit. In France, Germany, Italy, Holland, England, these groups of seekers are found through the centuries; they survive the times of darkness and clerical oppression. It would probably be a mistake to say that more than a very few of the 176 sects mentioned in *Gangroena* were spiritually minded people of this kind; but scattered all over England at the end of the Civil Wars were many groups of such mystics, known as Seekers. They were especially numerous in the districts that Fox saw with such startling clarity in his vision; and it was among the Seekers that the Quaker movement recruited the majority of its adherents. John Saltmarsh, an army chaplain and a deep thinker, wrote that 'they "wait" for power from on high, finding no practice of worship according to the first pattern'—i.e. finding that current forms of worship lacked the life of the Early Christian Church. 'They wait in prayer, pretending to no certain determination of things, nor to any infallible interpretation of Scripture. . . . They wait for an Apostle, or some one with a visible glory and power, able in the spirit to give visible demonstration of being sent.'[1] When they came to George Fox, these Seekers 'were led into the same first-hand experience that he himself enjoyed, so that they found their leader and teacher was not Fox but Christ'.[2]

As will be seen below, when we come to study Fox's *Journal*, he never had any other purpose than to turn people aside from the authority and systems of man, to lead them to God or to his

[1] Quoted by Rufus M. Jones, *Studies in Mystical Religion* (London, 1909), p. 456, from Saltmarsh's *Sparkles of Glory* (London, 1647).

[2] Edward Grubb, *What is Quakerism?* (London, 1917), p. 27.

Principles of that People Chosen by God and in Scorn called Quakers. So that all in all Christendom may read, and think upon their own Conditions. Set forth by George Fox (1662). *Latin was, as much as English, the language of controversy.*

PRINCIPIA

Quædam illius

Electi a Deo Populi,

Ironice nominati

QUAKERS.

Ut omnes per totum Christianismum legant,
& animadvertant suas ipsorum
Conditiones.

Exhibita per *Georgium Fox.*

LONDINI,
Pro *Roberto Wilson,* MDCLXII.

Christ—two names which for him implied one and the same reality. 'I was glad that I was commanded to turn people to that inward light . . . to bring people off from . . . their churches, which men had made, and gathered to the Church in God . . . to know the Spirit of Truth . . . (p. 35).

Professor Rufus M. Jones has remarked that Fox 'began at first as a "voice" crying in the rural districts, but he soon became a personal leader, an organizer and a vital interpreter— a prophet, in fact—of the mystical and seeking groups which abounded in the land. . . . He rendered conscious, explicit and visible in an organized form what had been vague and more or less subconscious.'[1] The early Quakers did in fact feel that they were rediscovering primitive Christianity, as it was when the Church organization and hierarchy did not exist, and when the sole qualification for membership of the Christian group was the leading of one's own heart. The Protestant reforms, arising straight out of Catholicism, represented an entirely different position. George Fox never thought he was founding a new church or sect; he was convinced that he had rediscovered a fundamental truth and that he preached 'the Truth'. It must be remembered that he did not use this word 'Truth' in any exclusive sense, and that he never believed himself infallible. The Truth was to him God speaking directly to the human soul without a human intermediary. He thought that no faith was real unless born out of personal experience. The Truth was religion-in-life, relegating human dogmas to a position of minor importance.

[1] Introduction to *Journal* (Everyman's Library edn., edited by Norman Penney. Dent, 1924).

The Parish Church at Fenny Drayton, Leics.

George Fox: His Early Years

George Fox was born in July 1624 in the little village of Drayton-in-the-Clay (now called Fenny Drayton) in Leicestershire. His father, Christopher, nicknamed by his neighbours 'righteous Christer', was a weaver, and was also a churchwarden. His mother, 'accomplished above most of her degree in the place where she lived', was a woman of deep religious sincerity; and some of her ancestors had gone to the stake for their Protestant faith. She always showed a kindly understanding for the 'gravity, wisdom and piety that very early shined through'[1] her son. It may have been her resistance that prevented relatives from pushing the young man into becoming a minister of the Established Church. The Foxes had five or six children whom they brought up in the fear of the Lord.

Here are the words of George Fox himself, taken from the

[1] William Penn, Preface to Fox's *Journal* (1694).

opening pages of his autobiographical *Journal*, which was first published in 1694, some three years after his death.

In my very young years I had a gravity and stayedness of mind and spirit not usual in children, insomuch that, when I have seen old men carry themselves lightly and wantonly towards each other, I have had a dislike thereof risen in my heart, and have said within myself, 'If ever I come to be a man, surely I should not do so nor be so wanton.'

When I came to eleven years of age, I knew pureness and righteousness; for while I was a child I was taught how to walk to be kept pure. The Lord taught me to be faithful in all things, and to act faithfully two ways, viz. inwardly to God and outwardly to man; and to keep to 'yea' and 'nay' in all things [i.e. keep strictly to the truth]. Afterwards, as I grew up, my relations thought to have me a priest,[1] but others persuaded to the contrary; whereupon I was put to a man, a shoemaker by trade, and that dealt in wool, and used grazing, and sold cattle; and a great deal went through my hands. While I was with him, he was blessed; but after I left him he broke, and came to

'*I was put to a man, a shoemaker by trade.*'

nothing. I never wronged man or woman in all that time, for the Lord's power was with me and over me, to preserve me. While I was in that service, I used in my dealings the word 'verily', and it was a common saying among people that knew me, 'If George says "Verily" there is no altering him.' When boys and rude people would laugh at me, I let them alone and went my way, but people had generally a love to me for my innocency and honesty (pp. 1–2).

While tending his master's flocks in the fields and meadows he had leisure to yield himself to the attraction of meditating and reading the Bible.

Meanwhile he was all the time observing and pondering the

[1] Here and elsewhere in the *Journal* the word priest is applied to all persons who were in receipt of money for preaching, irrespective of the particular sect to which they belonged.

religion of his fellow citizens. We do not know to what extent Fox learnt to mend shoes; among his contemporaries, both friendly and hostile, he was always spoken of as a cobbler, and the name stuck.

Through the many letters he wrote during the course of his life and also by his very numerous allusions to nature, we can appreciate how sane and attractive was his power over those who heard him.

An incident of secondary importance made him give up his trade. One market day, his cousin Bradford and a friend, having invited him into a tavern, wished to stay on and drink to excess; the one who gave up first was to pay for all three of them. George stood up, threw down a groat—his share—on the table, and went out. He was extremely grieved to see this inconsistency

'*The Tavern*' (1680).

in the Puritans. He spent the following night in prayer and weeping.

> The Lord . . . said unto me, 'Thou seest how young people go together into vanity and old people into the earth; and thou must forsake all, both young and old, and keep out of all, and be as a stranger unto all.'

Then at the command of God, on the 9th day of the Seventh Month, 1643, I left my relations and brake off all familiarity or fellowship with young or old. [He set out for Lutterworth, Northampton, Newport Pagnell, and Barnet.] As I thus travelled through the countries [i.e. counties], professors[1] took notice and sought to be acquainted with me, but I was afraid of them for I was sensible they did not possess what they professed. . . . From Barnet I went to London, where I took a lodging, and was under great misery and trouble there, for I looked upon the great professors of the city of London, and I saw all was dark and under the chain of darkness (pp. 3–4).

At another time it was opened in me that God, who made the world, did not dwell in temples made with hands. This, at the first, seemed a strange word because both priests and people use to call their temples or churches, dreadful places, and holy ground, and the temples of God. But the Lord showed me, so that I did see clearly, that he did not dwell in these temples which men had commanded and set up, but in people's hearts . . . his people were his temple, and he dwelt in them. . . .

After this I met with a sort of people that held women have no souls, adding in a light manner, no more than a goose. But I reproved them and told them that was not right, for Mary said, 'My soul doth magnify the Lord, and my spirit hath rejoiced in God my Saviour.' . . .

Now though I had great openings, yet great trouble and temptation came many times upon me. . . .

About the beginning of the year 1647, I was moved of the Lord to go into Derbyshire [then into other parts, without being able to find peace or even relief from his spiritual anguish. He was often under a great sense of strain]. I fasted much, and walked abroad in solitary places many days, and often took my Bible and went and sat in hollow trees and lonesome places till night came on; and frequently in the night walked mournfully about by myself, for I was a man of sorrows in the times of the first workings of the Lord in me.

Now during all this time I was never joined in profession of religion with any, but gave up myself to the Lord, . . . and travelled up and down as a stranger in the earth, which way the Lord inclined my heart . . . seeking heavenly wisdom and getting knowledge from the Lord . . . and was sometimes brought into such an heavenly joy that I thought I had been in Abraham's bosom. . . . Oh, the everlasting love of God to my soul when I

[1] In the *Journal* 'professors' means those who profess any kind of religion.

. . . whilst yet another flew into a mad rage because Fox had inadvertently stepped on the edge of a flower-bed in his garden. From the engraving by Robert Spence.

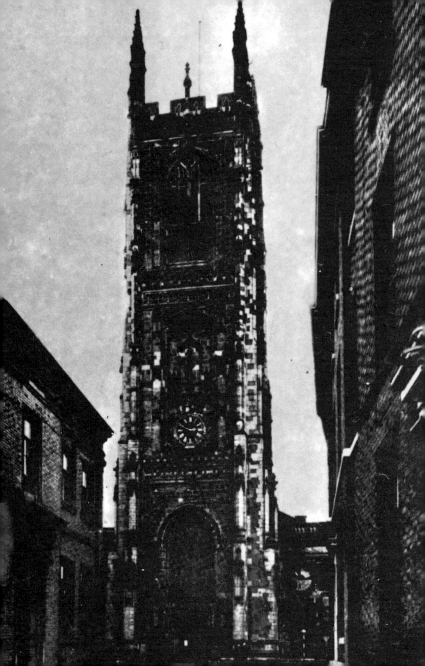

was in great distress! When my troubles and torments were great, then was his love exceeding great. . . .

And when all my hopes in them and in all men were gone, so that I had nothing outwardly to help me, nor could tell what to do, then, Oh then, I heard a voice which said, 'There is one, even Christ Jesus, that can speak to thy condition', and when I heard it my heart did leap for joy (pp. 8–11).

Let us consider, in parenthesis, this quotation from William James's lecture on George Fox in *Varieties of Religious Experience*, showing how spiritual life breaks in upon the human soul.

The Religious experience . . . is that which lives itself out within the private breast. First-hand individual experience of this kind has always appeared as a heretical sort of innovation to those who witnessed its birth. Naked comes it into the world and lonely; and it has always, for a time at least, driven him who had it into the wilderness, often into the literal wilderness out of doors, where the Buddha, Jesus, Mohammed, St. Francis, George Fox, and so many others had to go. George Fox expresses well this isolation . . . referring to the period of his youth when religion began to ferment within him seriously. . . . A genuine first-hand religious experience like this is bound to be a heterodoxy to its witnesses, the prophet appearing as a mere lonely madman.

Fox was about twenty years of age when these 'exercises' came upon him; he says that he 'went to many a priest to look for comfort but found no comfort from them'. Finally he returned home, for he knew that his parents were grieved by his absence. They then tried to get him to marry, but he told them that he was still but a lad; others would have liked to see him enter the Parliament army; but he refused all such suggestions. He felt drawn to men of the Church, for he was hoping to find there an answer to his problems and his distress of soul. He asked them questions and argued with them, but they treated him as though he were ill, and one of them advised him to 'take tobacco and sing psalms'. Another, who was considered to be a man of experience, seemed to Fox 'like an empty hollow cask', whilst yet another flew into a mad rage because Fox had inadvertently

A 'steeple-house' at Derby, where Fox suffered his first imprisonment.

stepped on the edge of a flower-bed in his garden. He followed another's advice to let himself be bled: but he did not bleed. '[My] sorrows, grief, and troubles . . . were so great upon me that I could have wished I had never been born.'

About the beginning of the year 1646, as he was going to Coventry, a thought came to him concerning this saying: '. . . all Christians are believers, both Protestants and Papists; and the Lord opened to me that, if all were believers, then they were all born of God and passed from death to life, and that none were true believers but such. . . .' Making profession of Christian faith was not enough to make one a son of God.

Then, as he was walking in a field on a First-Day (Sunday) morning, 'the Lord opened to me that being bred at Oxford or Cambridge was not enough to fit and qualify men to be ministers of Christ'; this was, however, the common belief of people. He realized that this revelation struck at the very ministry of the priests; and he would go off alone with his Bible into orchards and fields. He had got to know the Scriptures so well that if they had been destroyed, Fox could, so it was said, have rewritten them from memory.

In this last vision, a revelation made to him directly and independently of what he might have heard or read, even in the Scriptures, we touch the very heart of Quakerism, the true starting-point of George Fox's preaching. To quote again from his *Journal* on this point: 'These things I did not see by the help of man, nor by the letter, though they are written in the letter, but I saw them in the light of the Lord Jesus Christ, and by his immediate Spirit and power, as did the holy men of God, by whom the Holy Scriptures were written.'

The note of personal discovery, the certainty of Truth inwardly revealed, is found in the writings of almost all the early Quakers. These men and women wrote in the fervour of a spiritual experience directly realized in their own souls. 'I have heard of thee by the hearing of the ear; but now mine eye seeth thee,' said Job (42 : 5). There is a great difference between hearing and even understanding a fact explained by someone else, and going through the same experience oneself.

'Did not our hearts burn within us . . . ?'
The Pilgrims at Emmaus, by Rembrandt (1648).

It is time to consider what is this 'Inner Light'—Quakers use interchangeably the terms Inner Light, Inward Light, and the Light Within—that has been spoken of in Quaker writings ever since the days of George Fox. It is not reason. It is not conscience. It is something different. People do not become Christians merely by reading the Gospels or blindly submitting to the authority of the Church. They only become Christians in so far as they feel it inwardly and have an intimate revelation of it, in an experience like that of the disciples on the Walk to

Emmaus: 'And their eyes were opened, and they knew him; and he vanished out of their sight. And they said one to another, Did not our heart burn within us, while he talked with us by the way, and while he opened to us the scriptures?' (Luke 24: 31–2). It is 'enlightenment' in its strongest sense which convinces us, to use a very poor word to describe such an uprush of feeling.

The Inner Light enables us to perceive the utter holiness of Jesus; by it we can understand intuitively—for intuition reaches farther than intellect—what manner of man Jesus was. By the Inner Light we come into the knowledge of God by Jesus Christ; for, as Jesus said, 'he that hath seen me hath seen the Father'. We can attain to no final knowledge of God by the road of conscience or intellectual argument. Such knowledge comes to us not only by observation of things about us, as in knowledge of the natural world; nor does it proceed solely from the testimony or teaching of the Bible or of groups of people in whom is vested the authority of the Church. All those things can merely help and prepare us to gain a true knowledge of God; but they cannot give it us until we reach the point of 'seeing' with our inward eye. 'You will say, Christ saith this, and the apostles say this; but what canst thou say? Art thou a child of Light, and hast thou walked in the Light, and what thou speakest, is it inwardly from God?' (Quoted by Margaret Fell, whom Fox was to marry in 1669.)

> From this conception, so strange to the seventeenth century, of a principle of God carrying its own assurance within every man, even in the heathen who knew not the Scriptures or Christ in the flesh, came Fox's teaching of the social and spiritual life of a Christian; and it is in the light of this that his acts and his messages are to be seen. This note of personal discovery, of the certainty of Truth inwardly revealed, is almost universal in the writings of the early Quakers.[1]

The Apostles believed they were guided by the spirit of their risen Lord, so that they might know what it was that they should do (Acts 13: 2–4; 16: 6–7). It was the same for the early Friends.

[1] A. Neave Brayshaw, *The Personality of George Fox* (London, 1933).

24

God had become a living reality in everyday life; and this belief in the Inner Light brought with it a stronger faith than is generally found among Christians. Whoever claims to follow Quaker Christianity must seek the guidance of the Spirit and endeavour to follow it in all the business of life. This does not mean seeking more or less 'supernatural' manifestations or visions or voices:

> rather, it is to be sought in the enlightening of the reason and conscience, and in the clearing of the judgement so that the facts that *ought* to influence a decision are clearly perceived and given their due weight . . . the Spirit guides by raising a man's personality to higher powers of insight and sound judgement. . . . It should be added that the process by which a good man decides on his course of action is never a purely intellectual one. Intellect may, in some measure, enable him to judge whether a particular line of action will or will not promote the end he has in view; but for deciding the much more vital question whether that end is a *worthy* one he needs some kind of Inward Light.[1]

Fox and the early Quakers spoke not only of the Light but also of the Seed that was in all mankind; the seed of God was in every man, of whatever nation or race he might be, whether believer, pagan or atheist. The Seed was in all, with its latent possibilities. It is the 'divine spark', to use a more modern term that is accepted in many Christian circles. George Fox would often be heard appealing to what is pure and good in man, for that is a manifestation of God. Setting one's life on the path of goodness is an essential way of reaching the knowledge of God. 'Dwell in that which is pure and eternal which guides the mind to God', such was the advice he was to give his followers, 'that ye may answer that of God in everyone', or 'answering the witness of God in everyone', so as to appeal to the good that is in him. Certain members of his movement had been taken prisoner and were being held to ransom at Algiers: Fox advised them to act in such a way that 'in your lives and conversations and words you may preach . . . the life of Truth, so that you may answer the Spirit of God, both in the Turks and Moors and the rest of the

[1] Grubb, op. cit., pp. 46–7.

captives'. He was protesting against the then universally held belief that pagans were destined to eternal damnation.

One of the best-known passages relating to this principle occurs in a letter he wrote to Friends from his imprisonment at Launceston, where he endured the most horrible of all his spells of captivity. He asks them so to live 'that your carriage and life may preach among all sorts of people, and to them. Then you will come to walk cheerfully over the world, answering that of God in every one; whereby in them ye may be a blessing, and make the witness of God in them to bless you. Then to the Lord God you will be a sweet savour and a blessing.'

One of Fox's constant ideas, to which he returns again and again in his letters to his fellow disciples, is that they are bound up in the lives of one another. 'Know the life of God in one another, and the Power of God in one another.' 'Feel the power of God in one another.' 'Know one another in this love that changeth not.'

For Quakers, Christianity is essentially an experience of the light of Christ in the soul, and a way of life based on that experience. Jesus Christ came to bring spirit and life, and in intimate communion with the Creator they find the life that is to guide their lives.

This implies the rejection of all human barriers: the Church, the clergy, compulsory sacraments, unchangeable creeds, and even the 'letter' of the Scriptures; that is why Quakerism was condemned as the most frightful heresy. 'Let me show you,' said Dr. George Hickes, preaching to Oxford University, 'what a dangerous, damnable and precarious principle that is which asserts that immediate revelation or inspiration is not ceased, but is a standing and perpetual gift in the Church of Christ.' (*The Spirit of Enthusiasm Exorcised*, 1680.)

It is, however, obvious that such an attitude of liberty ran the risk of casting the movement into anarchy, not only at its birth during so troubled a period, but also later on, during the three centuries of its existence. Thanks to the good sense and the wisdom of Fox and his companions, this fatal danger was avoided, even in the early period. They succeeded in gently

26

disciplining men and women who were often comparatively un-educated, and in preventing them from compromising the Quaker movement. The early Quakers became aware that there can be a higher thing than individual inspiration, namely the check and balance of collective inspiration. This is not the control exercised by a kind of Sacred College as in Rome, but by the group of whom one is a member, in which all are equal in duties and rights. Neither Fox nor any of his companions ever assumed authority comparable, for example, to that of the superior in a monastery. He was never more than one amongst many, and he was careful not to indulge in any authoritarian actions to which popular enthusiasm might have led him. In organizing his Society, his ideal was that of a theocracy, where there would never be, and never has been, a president.

George Fox was twenty-two years of age when he had this mystical experience of discovering Christ in his soul. He was still to pass through doubts, and he says:

> I was in great perplexity and trouble for many days, yet I gave up myself to the Lord still. . . . And when at any time my condition was veiled, my secret belief was stayed firm, and hope underneath held me, as an anchor in the bottom of the sea, and anchored my immortal soul to its Bishop, causing it to swim above the sea, the world where all the raging waves, foul weather, tempests, and temptations are. . . .

> I saw also that there was an ocean of darkness and death, but an infinite ocean of light and love, which flowed over the ocean of darkness. In that also I saw the infinite love of God; and I had great openings (pp. 14, 19).

His Mission Begins

George Fox was twenty-three when we find him at Broughton in Leicestershire, taking part in a great meeting of Baptists, 'with some that had separated from them. . . . And the Lord opened my mouth. . . .' Henceforth the eyes of religious people were upon him. A dying man had visions of what Fox would achieve. 'Yet the work of the Lord went on in some . . . and tears of joy dropped from me. . . . I saw the harvest white, and the Seed of God lying thick in the ground, as ever did wheat that was sown outwardly, and none to gather it.' This vision was his consecration; from now on, he would never again doubt the will of his Lord.

In the following year, at Mansfield, where there was a great meeting, he was moved to pray, 'and the Lord's power was so great that the house seemed to be shaken'. He was asked to pray again, but he replied that he 'could not pray in man's will'.

At Leicester he had a great dispute with men belonging to different churches. They argued about what the Church was.

He asked the priest who was presiding over the meeting: '"Dost thou call this place a church? Or dost thou call this mixed multitude a church?" . . . I told him the Church was the pillar and ground of Truth, made up of living stones, living members, a spiritual household which Christ was the head of: but he was not the head of a mixed multitude, or of an old house made up of lime, stones, and wood. . . . There were several convinced that day . . . and the Lord's power and glory shined over all' (pp. 18 et seq.).

He held other great meetings in Nottinghamshire and then in Derbyshire; and for the first time we find the word 'Friends' used: '. . . there was a meeting of Friends, where there was such a mighty power of God. . . . And many were moved by the Lord to go to the steeplehouses, to the priests and to the people, to declare the everlasting Truth unto them' (p. 26).

Independently of Fox, the people were moving towards a religion of Spirit and of Life; and as this aspiration was so intensely alive in him, he made it clear and powerful for them. His message fell like a burning spark into their waiting hearts.

Many were turned from the darkness to the light within the compass of these three years, 1646, 1647, and 1648. And divers meetings of Friends, in several places, were then gathered to God's teaching, by his light, spirit, and power. . . . All things were new, and all the creation gave another smell unto me than before, beyond what words can utter. . . . And I was at a stand in my mind whether I should practise physic for the good of mankind, seeing the nature and virtues of the creatures were so opened to me by the Lord . . . but as people come into subjection to the spirit of God, and grow up in the image and power of the Almighty, they may receive the Word of wisdom, that opens all things, and come to know the hidden unity in the Eternal Being (pp. 27, 28).

And I was to direct people to the Spirit that gave forth the Scriptures, by which they might be led into all Truth, and so up to Christ and God, as they had been who gave them forth. . . . For I saw that Christ had died for all men, and was a propitiation for all, and had enlightened all men and women with

his divine and saving light, and that none could be a true
believer but who believed in it. . . . These things I did not see
by the help of man, nor by the letter, though they are written
in the letter, but I saw them in the light of the Lord Jesus
Christ, and by his immediate Spirit and power, as did the holy
men of God, by whom the Holy Scriptures were written. Yet
I had no slight esteem of the Holy Scriptures, but they were
very precious to me, for I was in that spirit by which they were
given forth, and what the Lord opened in me I afterwards
found was agreeable to them (p. 34).

Here is the very characteristic passage from his autobiography,
concerning what he felt to be his mission in the world:

Now, when the Lord God and his son, Jesus Christ, did send
me forth into the world, to preach his everlasting gospel and
kingdom, I was glad that I was commanded to turn people to
that inward light, spirit, and grace, by which all might know
their salvation, and their way to God; even that divine Spirit
which would lead them into all Truth and which I infallibly
knew would never deceive any. But with and by this divine
power and spirit of God, and the light of Jesus, I was to bring
people off from all their own ways to Christ, the new and living
way, and from their churches, which men had made and
gathered, to the Church in God, the general assembly written
in heaven, which Christ is the head of . . . and to be led thereby,
that in it they might worship the Father of spirits, who seeks
such to worship him, which spirit they that worshipped not in
knew not what they worshipped.

And I was to bring people off from all the world's religions,
which are vain, that they might know the pure religion, and
might visit the fatherless, the widows and the strangers, and
keep themselves from the spots of the world. [Epistle of
James 1: 27.] And then there would not be so many beggars,
the sight of whom often grieved my heart, to see so much hard-
heartedness amongst them that professed the name of Christ.
And I was to bring them off from all the world's fellowships,
and prayings, and singings, which stood in forms without
power, that their fellowships might be in the Holy Ghost, and
in the eternal Spirit of God; that they might pray in the Holy
Ghost, and sing in the spirit and with the grace that comes by
Jesus. . . .

An Anglican service about 1700.

'I was glad that I was commanded to turn people . . . from their churches, which men had made and gathered. . . .'

And I was to bring people off from Jewish ceremonies, and from heathenish fables, and from men's inventions and windy doctrines, by which they blowed the people about this way and the other way, from sect to sect; and all their beggarly rudiments, with their schools and colleges for making ministers of Christ, who are indeed ministers of their own making but not of Christ's; and from all their images and crosses, and sprinkling of infants, with all their holy days (so called) and all their vain traditions, which they had gotten up since the apostles' days, which the Lord's power was against, and in the dread and authority thereof I was moved to declare against them all, and against all that preached and not freely, as being such as had not received freely from Christ (pp. 34–6).

The worldly spirit of the 'priests' made him suffer; and when he heard the bells ring to call worshippers to the 'steeple-houses', it struck him to the heart, 'for it was just like a market-bell to gather people together that the priest might set forth his ware to sale. Oh, the vast sums of money that are gotten by the trade they make of selling the Scriptures, and by their preaching . . . notwithstanding the Scriptures were given forth freely, and Christ commanded his ministers to preach freely' (p. 39).

To George Fox's way of thinking, a true minister receives his vocation and his inspiration direct from God; however important intellectual preparation may be, it only comes second. He believed in the need for ministers to mediate between God and man; but he also believed that *any* Christian may be called to minister to those whom God sends him. 'The Children of Light'—another name they gave themselves at the beginning of their existence—were fully aware of the presence of One who was in their midst during their religious meetings. It was to him that they deliberately left the direction of their gatherings. Feeling that they were all brothers, they could not possibly accept a human being to rule their worship and their conduct. George Fox used to refuse to speak until he was certain that it was under divine leading, for he considered that only then would his words have enough power to touch his hearers.

'God is a Spirit, and they that worship him, must worship him in spirit and in truth' (or as a modern version translates it: 'in spirit and in reality'). This worship could not be artificially constructed; and since Christ himself was their leader, they waited in silence to make it possible for him to guide them. A liturgy fixed in advance would have paralysed the liberty of the Spirit of God. Silence was not an end in itself, but a means to attain to communion with God, who was the goal of their worship. Silence made it easier to give and yield oneself up to the divine will. They were experiencing the 'real presence' of Christ when they were gathered together in his name, according to his promise; and it has well been said that no two Quaker meetings have ever been alike.

'For, when I came into the silent assemblies of God's people, I felt a secret power among them, which touched my heart; and as I gave way unto it I found the evil weakening in me and the good raised up', the theologian Robert Barclay wrote in 1676.

To each, then, was given the opportunity of developing the

gifts of God and of exercising the ministry to which each might be called. George Fox did not exclude women, considering that the two sexes were equal before God and could both be called by him to all forms of ministry. Their exclusion from spoken ministry in the Church was caused by a false interpretation of a single line of St. Paul, written in quite a different sense. In I Corinthians 11: 5, he says that if women 'pray or prophesy', they must have their heads covered.[1]

This way of public worship based on silence was one of the great innovations of George Fox and his companions. It obviously comes from their 'rediscovery' of the Inner Light, i.e. the possibility of immediate communion with God. Silent worship is probably much commoner among Quakers than in any other Christian body, and even today it is the most distinctive and most appreciated peculiarity of the Society of Friends.

In 1649 we find George Fox at Nottingham again. There he felt called to go into the church to give his testimony.

> And when I came there, all the people looked like fallow ground, and the priest, like a great lump of earth, stood in his pulpit above. He took for his text these words of Peter, 'We have also a more sure word of prophecy, whereunto ye do well that ye take heed, as unto a light that shineth in a dark place, until the day dawn, and the day-star arise in your hearts.' And he told the people that the Scriptures were the touchstone and judge by which they were to try all doctrines, religions, and opinions. . . . I . . . was made to cry out and say, 'Oh, no, it is not the Scriptures.' . . . But I told them what it was, namely, the Holy Spirit, by which the holy men of God gave forth the Scriptures . . . for it led into all Truth, and so gave the knowledge of all Truth. For the Jews had the Scriptures, and yet resisted the Holy Ghost, and rejected Christ . . . and took upon them to try their doctrines by the Scriptures, but erred in judgement, and did not try them aright, because they tried without the Holy Ghost. Now as I spoke thus amongst them, the officers came and took me away and put me into prison, a pitiful stinking place (pp. 39–40).

[1] See Grubb, op. cit., p. 64.

This first imprisonment was due not to Fox's speaking in church—it was at that time not unusual for members of the congregation to speak at the conclusion of the sermon—but to his giving way to zeal and impatience, and interrupting the service. The head sheriff, John Reckless, set him at liberty a short time later, and sent for him to his house, where they had 'great meetings'. Soon the sheriff with his wife and children became 'Friends'; and John Reckless, suddenly moved to go out and preach to the people, went out in his slippers and preached repentance in the market-place. Others followed his example, speaking to the mayor and the magistrates who, angered at it, sent for Fox from the sheriff's house and put him back in prison.

Then he turned again, and said, *You are a Rebel and a Traytor.* With that I struck my *Hand* on the *Table*, and told him I had *suffered* more than *Twenty* such as he, or any that was there: for I had been cast into *Derby-Dungeon* for *Six Months* together: and had *suffered much* because I would not take up *Arms* against this *King* before *Wooster-Fight*: and I had nothing but *Love* and *Good Will* to the *King.* *Did you ne're hear the like,* said *Middleton?* *Nay,* said I, *ye may hear it again if ye will.* For ye talk of the *King,* a *Company* of you: but where were ye in *Oliver's days?* and what did ye do for him then. So they tendered me the *Oath,* and I could not take it.
George Fox, his Journal (Ellwood Ms.)

SCRIPTIUNCULÆ
QUÆDAM
ANGLICO-LATINÆ,
Magiftratibus de Infula
MALTENSI,
Et *Imperatori Domus* de *Auftria* etiam et om-
nibus ejus *Principibus*; *Galliæ Regi*, et omnibus
Paeſtatibus ſub ejus ditione: *Hiſpanorum Regi*, et de-
nique *Romano Pontifici*, Exhibitæ.

SOME
PAPERS
Given forth in
ENGLISH & LATINE,
TO THE
MAGISTRATES
OF THE
Iſle of Milita,
And to the *Emperour* of the Houſe of *Auftria*,
and to all the *Princes* under Him. To the *King*
of *France* and to all the *Powers* that be under him:
To the *King* of *Spain*, and laſtly to the *Pope*.

By *George Fox.*
LONDINI, Pro *Roberto Wilſon*, apud officinam ejus ad Aquilam Nigram in *Martin l' Grand,* 1660.

Pamphlets by Fox, addressed to the magistrates of the Island of Malta and others protecting against violence, war, torture and imprisonment.

No sooner was he free than George Fox went on with his travelling and his preaching; but he was attacked, beaten, and stoned while in the stocks, so that when set free again he was 'scarce able to stand'.

During the year 1650, being at Derby, he was again arrested and closely questioned. The magistrates wanted to make him admit that he had no sin, like Christ. He answered, 'Sin! . . . Christ my Saviour hath taken away my sin, and in him there is no sin.' When asked if any of them were Christ, he replied, 'Nay, we are nothing, Christ is all.' However, he was con-demned to six months' imprisonment for blasphemy; but this

George Fox refuses to join the army. From the engraving by Robert Spence.

did not cool his zeal. From prison he wrote to the priests, to the magistrates, to his enemies, and to his friends.

As the time of his detention was coming to an end, officers tried to recruit him into the army with the rank of captain. They offered him, as a favour, a place in the army of the Republic, against the future Charles II. Fox replied that he knew 'from whence all wars did rise, even from the lust according to James's doctrine'; and that 'I lived in the virtue of that life and power that took away the occasion of all wars'. The discussion grew heated, and Fox was put into 'a lousy, stinking place low in the ground without any bed'. He spent another six months in gaol.

In such a short book as this, there is no room to discuss the history and development of Quaker pacifism, another characteristic of this religious movement. The principles of the Society of Friends were clearly set forth by the Declaration to Charles II (1660), which says, 'We . . . utterly deny . . . all outward wars and strife and fightings with outward weapons, for any end or under any pretence whatsoever . . . and we do certainly know, and so testify to the world, that the spirit of Christ, which leads us into all Truth, will never move us to fight and war against any man with outward weapons, neither for the kingdom of Christ, nor for the kingdoms of this world.' Ever since that time the Society has taken an unequivocal stand against war, declaring it to be incompatible with Christ's teaching of love and peace. Of course, in this question as in all others, each person must obey his own conscience; and, in England at least, no member has ever been disowned for having felt it his duty to join the armed forces. Again and again, during the wars of the past three centuries, the declarations against war have been restated.

To the *Pope*.

Friend, Read *this over and the sad La-
mentation that's over thee thou maist behold,
how that thy field is a field of blood, and how
that thou art naked, thy Emperors and thy Princes from the Spiritual Weapons, and the Armor
of God, who hast had the form but out of the Power since the Apostles dayes, for yet thee nor none
of thy Company durst ever adventure a meeting in
the field, with them that have the spiritual weapons,
(as in the book called the* Papists strength broken*)
Therefore thou and all the Emperors and Princes,
and thy self, having not the Spiritual Weapons,
and not the Armor of God, ye have been fain to set up
you Inquisitions, your Racks, your Tortures, your
Prisons, your Banishments, and this sheweth you
have no Rule nor Government by the Power of God,*
Therefore read this over that you may see what

EMPEROUR of CHINA,
his Subordinate KINGS
RINCES.

a *Power* above all *Powers*, and this *Power* is
it self manifest: And this is *God*, whose
is, who is an *Over-Ruler*, the *Creator*,
and *Maker* of all things in Heaven and
er the waters, and made the Sea,
aused it to bud, and bring forth;
easons in his hand; and placed
his being lost (his habitation) by
who is the *God of the Spirits of all*
breath and life of all mankind,
nd, *and would have all to know him,*
e in him, and to serve him, in the
God is Light, and this is the true
every man that cometh into the
on of God, the way to the father,
ages all people to *God*, that
od out of the earth, *Sin*, and
transgression: Now this is the
enlightened you withal; that doth
s, and the naughty words, and
nd your evil wayes you run into,
he *Light*, that doth discover all
enlightned you withal, *which is*
his *Light*, you receive Christ, you
e light discovers unrighteousness,
ions, of God, to receive this *Light*, you
omes from *unrighteousness*, and
into peace, and unity with God,
and

To the King of *FRANCE*.

*Read this over it concerns thy general
Good, and all the Powers that be under Thee, which are suitable things to
this present Age.*

Friend,

LEt none in all thy Dominion under *Thee*, be Imprisoned
till death, or persecuted, or Banished concerning *Religion, Church,* or *Ministry*, or about the *Scriptures,
Christ,* the *Apostles,* or *Saints* words, for such as do
so, are out of the life of *Christ,* the *Apostles,* and the *Saints.*
For all Christendom hath been on heaps, killing and destroying one another about the *Ministry, Church Worship,* and Scriptures, Killing, Imprisoning, and Banishing, Whipping, and
Torturing the bodies of men: Now the cause is, (that) Magistrates are out of the life of *Christ,* the *Prophets,* and the *Apostles,* and now into this is the *Lord God* bringing his people, to
wit, that which the Scriptures were given from, in which they
shall have unity, and fellowship with God, with the Scriptures
and with one another: Therefore is their so many Wayes, Opinions, and Judgments about the Scriptures, because they want
the *Spirit* that gave them forth, in which they shall all have
fellowship, and in which *is the bond of peace.*
George Bayly, was moved of the *Lord* to go over into *France,*
and was Imprisoned to death in *Paris,* whose innocent blood
will be required at your hands, and lies upon your heads. You
should have overcome evil with good, You should heape coals of
fire upon your Adversaries heads, You should love Enemies, let
them

*Friends carried such messages from Fox into
many countries. They did not reach China.*

His First Followers—
Swarthmoor Háll

In 1651, at the beginning of winter, Fox was released after a year's imprisonment. He immediately set out on his journeys again, going from town to town, from village to village, in his home county of Leicester, and then in Yorkshire, organizing meetings wherever there were men to listen to him. He followed his inspiration and the call of his first supporters, preaching in squares, market-places, cemeteries, and outside churches. Usually he was treated as a busybody, for he set no store by the titles that men gave themselves. He was unwilling to make any distinction between superiors and inferiors, and he began to thee-and-thou everyone: the singular pronoun was still in general use; the plural 'you' when addressed to one person smacked of class distinction; and he did this in order to show inward sincerity and the equality of men before God. He bowed to nobody and only removed his hat in prayer: this, in an age that set great store by these formalities. He treated Cromwell as man to man when he met him in Hyde Park or was invited to his palace. The Protector was sensible enough to accept these peculiarities, but noble lords and ordinary folk found them hard to stomach.

In the district of Selby and Beverley, he often enjoyed the hospitality of Justice Hotham. This man shared Fox's likes and dislikes; for some time Fox used his house as his headquarters, setting out thence in various directions. One day he went to a

> steeplehouse . . . where [the great high priest, their doctor] preached, and sat me down . . . till the priest had done. And he took a text, which was, 'Ho, every one that thirsteth, let him come freely, without money and without price.' And so I was moved of the Lord God to say unto him, 'Come down, thou deceiver and hireling, for dost thou bid people come freely and take of the water of life freely, and yet thou takest three hundred

38   *'Here are my leather breeches which frighten all the priests and professors.*
From the engraving by Robert Spence

pounds off them for preaching the Scriptures to them. . . . Did not Christ command his ministers, "Freely you have received, freely give"?' And so the priest, like a man amazed, packed away (p. 76).

Fox then had plenty of time to speak to the people, to direct them 'from darkness to the light and to the spirit of God their free teacher'.

Several Yorkshire priests became his followers and renounced all taxes and tithes. Fox was often beaten and hounded out, but went on with his ministry undeterred. He knew that the apostle Paul had worked with his hands to supply his own needs. Fox, too, never accepted money from anyone and, like St. Francis of Assisi, he practised detachment and poverty, without however becoming a beggar. In any case he had a small patrimony; and he had made himself leather breeches, because this material was simple and durable. To those who did not know him by name, he was 'the man in leather breeches'.

One day he came to a town, and a great meeting was held in the open air, to which professing Christians of various persuasions had come in order to argue with him. 'And I sat of a

nd there was a Captain stoude uppe after ye Meeting was donne and asked mee where my Leather Britches was and I lett ye Man run a swile and att last I holde uppe my Coate and saide 'Heere is my Leather Britches which frighten all ye Priests and Professors'.

George Fox his Journal.

haystack and spoke nothing for some hours for I was to famish them from words. . . . And at last I was moved of the Lord to speak, and they were all reached by the Lord's power . . . and there was a general convincement amongst them' (p. 88). At Balby, Fox and some of his companions were stoned down the streets; the following Sunday, at Tickhill, he went into the church to speak; 'and the clerk up with his Bible as I was speaking and hit me in the face that my face gushed out with blood'. He was dragged out of the church, stoned, beaten, thrown over a hedge into a garden, beaten, thrown back again, till he was smeared all over with blood and dirt. But 'my spirit was revived again by the power of God' and 'I declared to them the word of life and showed to them . . . how they dishonoured Christianity.' Later, the man who had shed Fox's blood in the

church was afraid that he would have his hand cut off 'for striking me in the steeplehouse', but Fox forgave him, and would not appear against him at the judicial inquiry.

As they travelled, Fox and his companions came near a great hill called Pendle Hill. (Its evil reputation for witches is still known in the villages round about.) He climbed to the top, and saw the vision described at the beginning of this book.

Some days later, Fox went up into the fells at Firbank in Westmorland and sat down on a rock overlooking the valley. For about three hours he spoke,

Pendle Hill, Lancashire.

George Fox on Pendle Hill, 1652.
'. . . . and there on the top, I was moved to sound the day of the Lord.*

As we travelled on, we came near a very great and high *Hill*, called *Pendle Hill*, and I was moved of the *Lord*, to go to the Top of it; which I did with much adoe Itt was soe very *Steepe* and *High*. When I came a'toppe of Itt I saw the *Lancasheere Sea*; and there atoppe of the *Hill* I was moved to sounde ye *Day* of ye [*Lorde*] and ye *Lorde* lett mee see a'toppe of ye *Hill* in what *Places* hee had a *Great People* to be gathered. And see on ye *Hills syde* I founde a *Springe* and refresht my selfe; for I had eaten and drunk little for severall *Days*.

Fox's Pulpit is again a meeting-place for Quakers.

on that Sunday afternoon, to a crowd of over a thousand people, directing them to the Spirit of God in themselves. Many 'Separate teachers' were converted—i.e. teachers in congregations of Seekers who had separated themselves from all religious bodies—and they joined him forthwith.

In the spring of that same year, Fox made his first journey to Swarthmoor, near Ulverston. This was the home of worthy Judge Fell, the vice-chancellor of Lancaster, who twenty years previously had married Margaret Fell. Ever since then, their home had been a place of hospitality for friends and strangers. The judge was away on circuit when Fox came to Swarthmoor, but he was welcomed with open arms and was grateful for so much kindness. On the day after he arrived, Fox had an un-pleasant encounter with the priest of Ulverston; he was put out of the church and it was only thanks to Margaret Fell that he was allowed to go on with his speaking in the graveyard. The judge, having heard of this little affray, came home very ill-pleased; but

◀ *Firbank Fell. On the right, among the scattered trees, is the rock now known as Fox's Pulpit. The Lune Valley runs down to the right, between Fox's Pulpit and the far-ther range of hills.*

a conversation with Fox made him so at ease in his mind that he gladly put his house at Fox's disposal. Until his death in 1658 he was a great help to the new Society, taking up its defence against his colleagues on the bench.

So Swarthmoor became the centre of the young movement. Quaker preachers came there for rest and refreshment, and also to recuperate, for they were only too frequently beaten up. Under Margaret Fell's direction it was also a centre of information. She maintained a regular correspondence with the itinerant preachers and with those in prison. Eighteen years later, and ten years after the death of Judge Fell, Fox, with the agreement of his followers and of Margaret Fell's children, married the lady of Swarthmoor.

With the year 1653 a new era of intense religious activity began. Numerous preachers, drawn from all ranks of society— merchants, farmers, former ministers of the Church, people of small means—would thenceforth be accompanying George Fox on his journeys or would take his teaching up and down England and as far as America. Known as the First Publishers of Truth, these missionaries, who have been called the Valiant Sixty, spread in 1654 throughout England, Scotland, and Ireland. They knew that they would encounter opposition, imprisonment, and possibly death, but they were ready to suffer in the cause of Christ.

At Ulverston a wild mob attacked Fox and beat him senseless. After lying unconscious for quite a time, he gradually came to, then 'stood up again in the eternal power of God' with the people all about him and, stretching out his arms to the crowd, he said with a loud voice, 'Strike again, here is my arms and my

Swarthmoor Hall, the home of Margaret Fell and of the movement in its early days.

head and my cheeks'; and suddenly, filled with strength, he began to 'declare unto them the word of life'. When he came back to Swarthmoor, he found the Friends dressing the heads and hands of those who had been injured that day 'by the professors and hearers' of the priest. Another day, when he was with James Nayler, they were nearly thrown into the sea and were again cruelly beaten. Being accused of blasphemy, Fox went of his own accord to the sessions at Lancaster. Forty priests fell over each other to tell lies about him. To one of them who said that the Spirit and the letter were inseparable, he replied, '. . . then every one that has the letter has the spirit and they may then buy the spirit with the letter of the Scriptures'. After Judge Fell had intervened, Fox was acquitted. In Westmorland, where he held several meetings, he had occasion to point out to a priest who said that the Scriptures are *the* Word of God, that they are only the 'words of God', since it is Christ who is the Word, according to John.

Fox's pulpit.

It is now time to say a few words about those fine people who, from 1652 onwards, joined George Fox in his spiritual labours. The Society of Friends being based on the doctrine of the Inner Light, that 'Light which lighteth every man that cometh into the world', one can only get to know the movement well by studying the men who have lived in it and have made it what it is. It has never relied on dogmas or on large numbers, but on Christian character in the individual; thus it depends entirely on the spiritual life of its members. Their consecration takes the place of the creeds and official statements that we find elsewhere. Conscience and the way of living are the most important things about Quakerism.

These men and women who responded to the call of Fox were necessarily mystics who had already been through deep experiences. Amongst these we should mention Isaac and Mary Pennington, who belonged to the upper classes; Isaac was imprisoned six times during his life (1616–79). There was James Nayler, who died in 1660; Edward Burrough and Richard Hubberthorne, who both died in Newgate Prison in London, in 1662 and 1663; Francis Howgill, formerly a minister (1618–68); William Dewsbury (1621–88); James Parnell, who died in gaol at the age of nineteen, in 1655; Margaret Fell, the future wife of George Fox (1614–1702); Mary Dyer, put to death at Boston, Massachusetts, in 1660; Mary Fisher and Ann Austin, whose books were burnt and who were themselves imprisoned when they landed at Boston; Catherine Evans and Sarah Chevers, who were imprisoned in Malta by the Inquisition and kept there for three appalling years; and finally the two who are the best-known:

46

Mary Fisher, one of Fox's first followers, speaking to the Sultan of Turkey in 1657.

William Penn (1644–1718) and Robert Barclay (1648–1690). William Penn will be dealt with separately in the chapter on the Quakers in America, as he is best known for his foundation of Pennsylvania and the city of Philadelphia.

Robert Barclay was born in Scotland and joined Fox when he was in his early twenties. He has been called 'the great Scottish theologian', because of his work that appeared in Latin in 1676, entitled *Apology of the true Christian theology, professed and preached by those who are in derision called Quakers*, etc. This book was written in defence of Quaker doctrine, as a reply to the learned men of the time. It was afterwards translated into English, Dutch, and French. The *Apology* was frequently reprinted, and it was for a long time the best defence of the Quaker faith.

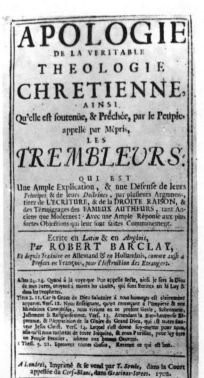

Title-page of the first French edition of the Apology—defence of Quaker theology—by Robert Barclay. 1702. The title-page of the original edition is on p. 157.

This was thought to be a portrait of George Fox. Until recently, it was attributed to the Court painter Sir George Lely. There is no authentic portrait of Fox.

His Character and Physical
Appearance—
Contemporary Accounts

'If I had to make a list of saints, I should include George Fox,'
said an English clergyman; and yet in the Christian world he
remained comparatively unknown, although he has so many
points in common with the greatest founders of religious orders:
powerful personality, mysticism, gift of healing, genius for
organization.

To judge by contemporary accounts, George Fox was tall and
strong; his mighty voice made him perfectly audible for hours
on end when he was speaking in the open air to thousands of
people. His clear, penetrating eyes seemed to search the very
depths of one's soul. His hair was long, with a parting down the
middle. He had a long nose, but his mouth was rather small, if
we accept a portrait of very dubious authenticity, formerly
attributed to the Court painter, Sir Peter Lely.

'To hear Fox preach once in the churchyard as he passed
through the town, or to spend an evening with him by the fire-
side, often was enough to change a persecutor into an en-
thusiast, to emancipate a man from the intellectual and social
customs of a lifetime.'[1]

He had personal magnetism that attracted people to him;
Penn and Barclay (men of learning), Pennington and Ellwood
(men of quality), shopkeepers, farmers, poor people, all had
deep affection for him, which lasted long after he had gone from
this world.

He knew the Bible thoroughly; but he was never able to write
without making crude spelling mistakes, like most of his contemporaries. It is known that his *Journal* and his other works

[1] G. M. Trevelyan, *England under the Stuarts* (London, 1928), pp.
312–13.

The Geneva Bible (1614 edition). The Bible was becoming so familiar to English people that 'a boy that driveth the plough' would know it well.

were dictated to kind-hearted secretaries, even during his journeys. He showed a naïve pride in his knowledge of Hebrew, Welsh, and Greek: this was one of his weaknesses. He owed his personal ascendancy, above all, to his patience in the face of insults and even blows, for he was convinced that he had to 'answer that of God in everyone'. The force of his personality, rather than his actual eloquence, drew the crowds, for he knew nothing of the art of oratory.

Professor Rufus M. Jones wrote in 1924:

> One of the outstanding features of his spiritual mission was his clear, sure insight into the moral and social condition of his time. His proposed remedy may not always seem sound and adequate to a generation that has had the advantage of scientific training in social problems, but it is interesting to see how Fox puts his finger with almost infallible certainty upon the sore spots and the evil tendencies around him. He was as tender as a mother over all who were victims—and what a list it was and

Cunctis, Viam in

REGNUM,

Noscere Desiderantibus, sint vel
in Formis extra Formas,
vel omnibus Formis
Superiores.

Admonitio

Mentes vestras ut introrsum, ubi
vox Domini (quem quasi remotum,
inscienter adoratis) audienda est,
invertatis; illumque ibi vera pro Sapi-
entia expectare.

Veritatem ab errore, verbum a litera, po-
tentiam a forma, veras denique, a falsis,
Prophetas ut possicis decernere.

Ab illis Edita, quos mundus TREMENTES,
Contemptim denominatur.

Authore Georgio Fox.

LONDINI, Pro Roberto Wilson, apud officinam
ejus ad Aquilam nigram in Martins † Grand 1660.

. To all that would

Know the Way
TO THE
KINGDOME,

Whether they be { In Forms,
{ Without Forms, or
{ Got above all Forms.

A Direction to turn your minds within, where the voice of God is to be heard,
whom you ignorantly worship as afar off; and
to wait upon him for the true Wisdome.

That you may know Truth from Errour, the
Word from the Letter, the Power from the Form,
and the true Prophets from the false.

Given forth by those whom the world in scorn calls
QUAKERS.

By G. F.

The fourth Edition corrected and amended.

LONDON, Printed for Robert Wilson at the Black-Spread-
Eagle and Wind-Mill, in Martins † Grand, 1660.

Another pamphlet by George Fox.

still is!—of man's brutality, injustice, stupidity, greed or care-
lessness. He hated every artificial fashion which contracted the
full human life of any man or woman. He went about his task
of liberating men and transforming society with an absolute
confidence in God's guidance and in the power of His Spirit,
and with an unlimited faith in human possibilities, and in the
effectiveness of the spirit of sincere love and kindness when put
full into practice.[1]

William Penn, in his preface to the first edition of Fox's
Journal (1694), said:

His ministry and writings show they are from one that was
not taught of man. . . . Nor were they notional or speculative,
but sensible [understandable] and practical truths, tending to
conversion and regeneration and the setting up of the kingdom
of God in the hearts of men. . . . He had an extraordinary gift
in opening the Scriptures. He would go to the marrow of
things. . . . But above all he excelled in prayer. The inwardness

[1] Introduction to the Everyman's Library edition of Fox's *Journal*.

51

and weight of his spirit, the reverence and solemnity of his address and behaviour, and the fewness and fulness of his words, have often struck even strangers with admiration, as they used to reach others with consolation. . . . So meek, contented, modest, easy, steady, tender, it was a pleasure to be in his company. He exercised no authority but over evil, and that everywhere and in all; but with love, compassion, and long-suffering. A most merciful man, as ready to forgive as unapt to take or give an offence. . . . He held his place in the Church of God with great meekness and a most engaging humility and moderation. . . . I write my knowledge and not report, and my witness is true, having been with him for weeks and months together on divers occasions. . . . Civil, beyond all forms of breeding, in his behaviour; very temperate, eating little and sleeping less, though a bulky person. . . . So full of assurance was he, that he triumphed over death; and so even to the last, as if death were hardly worth notice or a mention. . . . And to some that came in and inquired how he found himself, he answered, 'Never heed, the Lord's power is over all weakness and death; the Seed reigns, blessed be the Lord.'

The Lord [was] pleased in his day to make great use of him and to do great things by him . . . of which there yet remain clouds of witnesses. (George Whitehead's Preface to Fox's *Epistles*, 1698.)

'In Journeyings Often . . .
In Prisons More Frequent'

After six or seven years' journeying up and down England, Fox was concerned to go to Scotland, to which country he had felt drawn for some time. He carried out his plan in 1657, setting off for the north accompanied by Robert Widders, 'a thundering man against hypocrisy and deceit, and the rottenness of the priests'. His coming made the Scottish clergy boil over; there were great meetings in the churches, and petitions against him were sent to the Council that Oliver Cromwell held at Edinburgh at that time. Fox went to that city, and held several large and stormy meetings. Summoned before the Council, he found them unwilling to listen to his reasons for coming to Scotland, and was given seven days to be out of the country. After Edinburgh, he went to Heads, in Lanarkshire, where Friends were being persecuted by the Presbyterian ministers; they were not being allowed to buy or sell anything, or eat and drink with anyone. After other visits, he went back to Edinburgh, although his seven days' grace had expired. When, at Leith, he was told that he would probably be arrested, he replied: 'What! do you tell me of their warrants against me? If there were a cartload of them I do not heed them, for the Lord's power is over them all.' After a meeting where 'the everlasting power of God was set over the nation', Fox and his companion returned to England without any mishap.

In 1669 he felt 'moved of the Lord' to go to Ireland. He set out with four of his followers and landed at Dublin. They visited several groups of Friends. At Cork, a great number of Friends were in prison, for the mayor was 'very envious against the Truth', and had issued four warrants to take Fox. Yet all their designs against him were defeated, for meetings were very large, Friends coming to them from far and near. When it was time for them to return to England, they went on board ship and spent two nights at sea; during one of them a violent storm arose that put the vessel in great danger, and, said Fox, 'I was fain to watch the winds as I had watched the tory [i.e. Irish] priests. And the same power of the Lord God which carried me over brought me back again.'

George Fox's most important journey was to America, from 1671 to 1673. Twelve members of the Society of Friends went with him. 'Our yacht', he says, 'was counted a very swift sailer. But she was very leaky, so that the seamen and passengers did, for the most part, pump day and night, which was good to keep seamen and passengers in health.' They had been at sea about three weeks when they were nearly attacked by pirates; the wind freshened in the night, and the pirates lost track of them. Fox was not seasick, but the hardships he had endured previously made him very ill during the voyage, and for three weeks after their landing at Barbados. His weak state did not prevent his taking part in numerous meetings of Friends and in organizing the life of the Society, particularly as regards marriages, births, burials and wills, and all 'other things relating to the affairs of the Church'. So far as their negroes were concerned, he 'desired them to endeavour to train them up in the fear of God . . . and to free them after thirty years' servitude'. Fox and his friends had many meetings that a few priests tried unsuccessfully to prevent.

After three months in Barbados, the little group left for Jamaica, where they stayed seven weeks. Meetings were 'large and very quiet'. The voyage from Jamaica to Maryland lasted nearly seven weeks, with a frightful storm near the end of it. They landed in Maryland just in time to attend a four days' meeting of Friends from all parts of the province. The English Friends then dispersed in various directions, 'for the service of Truth'. Fox sent to 'the Indian emperor and two of their kings' to come to a Meeting, and 'had in the evening two good opportunities with them. . . . They carried themselves very courteously and lovingly, and enquired where the next meeting would be.'

Travelling on horseback, he then set off for the north, towards New England, in order to take part in the 'half-year's meeting' of Friends at Oyster Bay on Long Island. It lasted four days. Soon after that, they sailed for Rhode Island, and attended the Yearly Meeting for all Friends in New England and the adjacent colonies; this lasted six days, the first four of which were devoted to large public meetings for worship. Afterwards they had other very fruitful meetings in various places, and Fox one day heard some magistrates saying among themselves that 'if they had money enough they would hire him to be their minister'. 'This was where they did not well understand us and our principles; but when I heard of it, I said, "It is time for me to be gone; for if their eye is so much on me, or any of us, they will not come to their own Teacher."' He travelled through the region again, and then returned to Maryland, where, after a long and difficult journey, he was able to take part in their General Meeting. One public meeting brought together over a thousand people: never had so many people been seen together in that country before. From Maryland he passed into Virginia, then to Carolina, back to Virginia, by boat or canoe, or on horseback along tracks interrupted by bogs and swamps. 'Now having travelled through most parts of that country . . . and had very good service for the Lord in America . . . we found our spirits begin to be clear of those parts of the world, and draw towards Old England again. . . . The same good hand of Providence that went with us, and carried us safely over, watched over us in our return, and brought us safely back again.'

In 1677 Fox prepared for a journey on the continent of Europe. He sailed for Holland, accompanied by William Penn, Robert Barclay and six other Friends. They had meetings at Rotterdam and Amsterdam, and during their stay they set up the organization of the Society of Friends in Holland and parts of north Germany. Fox travelled as far as Bremen and Hamburg. On their return to Holland they visited Leyden and The Hague, and got back to England after a difficult three days' passage. Fox was to return to Holland in 1684, but he only stayed a very short time.

For th

Friend

Who art the Chiefe Ruler of these Dominions, h
of God in scorne called Quakers, that have suffered under
been imprisoned, & suffered for conscience sake, & bearing
And these lyes yet in prison in ye Names of the Comm
Alsoe there hath dyed in Prison in ye Commonwealths
imprisonments nasty straw & dungeons ————
And there is imprisoned in thy name since thy Arriva
to thee by soe doing

And besides, ye Meetings are dayly broken up
in ye primitive times,) & are throwne into
where can hardly be uttered; & this wee we
of ye Comonwealth, & of ye two Protectors,
sake, who have not lifted up a hand against
rude people with their staves & swords & s

And one of ye greatest things that wee have suffered for
ments; And now are wee imprisoned becaus wee can

And now if oe yea be yea, & nay nay to thee, a
an Oath, for wee have suffered these many yeares both
sweare, but obey Christs Doctrine who commands wee
lives, & Estates, with oe yea & nay according to ye De

Harken to these things, & soe consider th
that hast ye Government that maist doe it

And an Account wee have more at large to shew of

Wee desire that all that are in prison m
for Conscience, & ye truths sake and
accusers be brought up before thee

A letter addressed to Charles II by George Fox, protesting against the imprisonment of more than 3,000 Quakers. This is the only complete signature of Fox that has survived.

King

is a list of some of ye Sufferings of the people
...changeable powers before this, of which there } 3173 Persons
...imony to ye truth as it is in Jesus
...ealth that wee know of   73 Persons
...livers & Richards time in their cruell and hard } 32 Persons
...by such as thought thereby to gratifie themselves } 3068 persons

...men wth Stubbs and Armes (wch meete peaceably according to ye people
...ers, C trodd upon till ye very blood gusk out of them, the number of
...have of thee, To set them at liberty that lye in prison in ye Names
...e in thy owne Name, for speaking ye truth, & for good conscience
...de, nor noe man, and that ye meetings might not be broken up by
...s, who peaceably meete together in ye feare of God to worshipp him.
...cause wee could not sweare to ye Protectors C all ye changeable Governe-
...take ye Oath of Alleageance.
...n upon ye Earth Let us suffer as much for breaking of that as for breaking
...lives C estates under these changeable Governments because we cannot
...d not sweare at all. Matth. 5. Jam. 5 And this we seal with our
...ine of Christ.
...in ye wisdome of God that with it such actions may be stopt then

...friends particular sufferings if required
...sofull liberty. And for ye time to come they may not be imprison-
...thou question the innocency of their sufferings, let them & their

...Witnesses of the truth of this who are
...Lovers of yr Soules, & your Eternall peace

To ye King
George ffox
Richard Hubberthorne

In his preface to the French edition of Fox's *Journal* (1935), Wilfred Monod wrote:

It is amazing to discover in these pages what daily heroism was involved by Fox's simple, Christian attitude in matters of conduct. With the sweetness of an angel he endured the long torture of insults, slander, threats, blows, wounds, fever, hunger and cold, sickness and infirmity, being imprisoned again and again in gaols that were smoky, wet, alive with vermin or stinking with excrement. He could have adopted other tactics, as he was no weakling: his powers of endurance showed that he was unusually strong, his voice could ring out above a roaring mob, and the keenness of his glance worried his adversaries and even made them 'quake'; but he would have no other weapon than the spirit of his Saviour, no other shield than prayer, no other banner than the Cross. What wonderful possibilities there are in the human heart! What supernatural capacities in the soul that is born again!

The first period of the history of the Society of Friends is marked by persecutions of all kinds. They were arrested in hundreds for refusing to pay tithes, to take off their hats to magistrates, or to swear loyalty to the government. Travelling preachers even had a law concerning vagabonds applied to them. Once arrested, they were left to rot in gaol for weeks without a trial. The cells were often dark, and were disgustingly filthy; the prisoners were soon crawling with lice, and had no bench to sit on nor mattress to lie on. In 1659 a petition signed by 164 Friends was presented to Parliament: the signatories asked to take the place of their brothers, in order to save them from almost inevitable death. The offer was of course refused. Francis Howgill spent five and a half years in prison, merely because he had refused to take the Oath of Allegiance. A young man of eighteen, James Parnell, when a jury had refused to convict him, was condemned to pay a fine of £40 or stay in prison in Colchester Castle. He was put in a cell like a baker's oven, only not so high; it had neither light nor air. His swollen legs would no longer carry him; he suffered for ten or eleven months with great patience, and died at the age of nineteen.

In America, the descendants of the Puritans who had fled

from English intolerance showed even greater intolerance and cruelty. This unspeakable behaviour amazed the Redskins, but did not prevent the Quakers from coming back repeatedly to evangelize North America.

In 1660, on the accession of Charles II, who had promised to grant liberty of conscience, 700 Friends were set free at the request of Margaret Fell. Soon, unfortunately, a special law was passed forbidding Friends to hold meetings of more than four persons, under pain of fine or banishment. Two years later, the Conventicle Act of 1664 aggravated the situation by making all Nonconformist churches illegal. Most of the Presbyterians and Baptists abandoned their places of worship and met secretly; Friends refused to obey and continued their meetings openly. Mass arrests followed. Several hundreds were banished and their properties sold.

Between 1661 and 1689, about 12,000 Quakers went to prison and more than 300 died there. (At Bristol, in 1682, most of the adult members being in prison, meetings were held by their children, with a calm and gravity above their years.) Their constancy and quiet firmness overcame their persecutors. In 1687 James II promulgated the Declaration of Indulgence, and in 1689, in the reign of William and Mary, the Toleration Act was passed, which granted liberty of worship to all Protestants. That was the end of the persecutions.

George Fox was in prison eight times, and for six years of his life. Prisons were until 1675 his only stopping-places on life's journey. The first time he was arrested was in 1649, at Nottingham, for interrupting a preacher in a church. He was set free again quite soon but, the next year, he was arrested at Derby for blasphemy and gaoled for six months. It was during this period that the justices gave leave that he should 'have liberty to go a mile. And I perceived their end, and I told the gaoler that if they would set me how far a mile was, I might walk in it sometimes, but it's like they thought I would go away. I told them I was not of that spirit.' His relatives offered to stand surety for him in the sum of £100, but Fox refused: he said he was 'innocent from any ill behaviour and had spoken the word of life and Truth unto them'. When he declined an offer to enter the army of Parliament, he was given an extra six months and thrown into a cell with thirty felons. In 1653 he was locked up at Carlisle for nearly two months 'as a blasphemer, a heretic, and a seducer'. The rumour went round that he was to be hanged; and he was guarded by three musketeers.

> And at nights they would let up priests . . . droves of them and exceeding rude and devilish they were. . . . But the Lord in his power gave me dominion over them all, and I let them see both their fruits and their spirits. . . . And great ladies and countesses came to see a man that they said was to die. . . . And there was a company of bitter Scottish priests and Presbyterians, made up of envy and malice, who were not fit to speak of the things of God, they were so foul-mouthed (p. 160).

He was transferred to a dungeon, with murderers and women 'put together in a nasty and very uncivil manner'; the prisoners were so lousy that one woman was almost eaten to death with lice. 'But the prisoners were made all of them very loving to me, and some of them were convinced.' The gaoler was very cruel; one day he came in and struck Fox with a great cudgel; 'and as he struck me I was made to sing in the Lord's power, and that made him rage the more'. Fox was at last set free at the request of the Short Parliament then in session.

In 1655 he was held for three weeks under suspicion of plotting against the government and holding Quaker meetings. Refusing to go home and stay there on parole, he was sent to London, escorted by an officer who took him to the Protector, Oliver Cromwell, at the palace of Whitehall. Their interview was a very courteous one. The Protector was soon convinced that Fox was a man of peace who would never take up arms against him. On being invited to stay to dinner in the great hall, he declined, which made Cromwell say, 'Now I see there is a people risen and come up that I cannot win either with gifts, honours, offices or places; but all other sects and people I can.' As they parted, the Protector caught Fox by the hand, and with tears in his eyes said, 'Come again to my house, for if thou and I were but an hour in a day together we should be nearer one to the other.'

All the *Talk* and *Cry* was, that I was to be *Hanged*. At *Night* they would bring up *Priests* to me, sometimes as late as the *Tenth Hour* in the *Night*; and they would be exceeding *Rude* and *Divellish*. *Great Ladies* also (as they were called) came to see the Man, that they said was to die ..... *Carlisle Prison.* 1653

G *Fox his Journal*.

Fox in prison at Carlisle in 1653.
From the engraving by Robert Spence.

In 1656 he was arrested during a preaching journey in Cornwall, and remained for eight months in a dungeon in Launceston. According to the custom of the time, the extortionate gaoler demanded from the prisoners seven shillings a week for feeding each of the horses of Fox and his two companions, and seven shillings more for the three prisoners. When they saw they were in for a long stay, they sent away their horses and ceased their payments to the gaoler; he then in his fury put them in Doomsdale, a dungeon of which it was said that few who went in ever came out alive. The excrement of the prisoners who had been put in it had not been cleaned out for years; the floor was all mire, and in places to the top of the shoes in water and urine. Some friendly people brought them a candle and a little straw, and they burnt a little of the straw to take away the stink. Later, Fox narrowly escaped being knifed by another prisoner, who had been encouraged by the gaoler to do it. (The following year this same gaoler was turned out of his place and put in Doomsdale where he had persecuted Fox. He died in prison and his family fell upon hard times.) At last, thanks to many efforts and to Cromwell's knowledge of the matter, they were set free.

In 1660 Fox, arrested at Swarthmoor and accused of plotting against the king, spent five months in Lancaster Castle. Many people came to see him, and he 'was moved of the Lord God to speak out of the gaol window to them and many people stood attentive to it. And I let them see how uncertain their religion was. . . .' Eventually the justices, to save money, let Fox go up to London unguarded, to have his case heard there. He appealed to the king and was set free.

In 1662, when the Quaker Act was passed, he was put in prison for a month on a charge of having intended to be present at a meeting, and for refusing to take the oath. His imprisonment at Lancaster and Scarborough lasted two years and eight months, from 1664 to 1666. Knowing that he was going to be arrested, Fox could have fled, but he did not want his escape to recoil upon Friends. The excuse was the rumour of a plot against the king: this charge was quickly disposed of, but the judge invited him to take the Oath of Allegiance; Fox refused, so that he might obey the solemn command in the Sermon on the Mount: 'Swear not at all', and the echo of it in the Epistle of James (5: 12): 'Swear not, neither by heaven, neither by the earth, neither by any other oath: but let your yea be yea; and your nay, nay.' Fox was then put in a tower, where the smoke of the other rooms came up so thick that sometimes he could hardly see the candle when it burned, and he was almost suffocated. Besides, it rained in upon his bed, and the violent winter wind kept blowing his window open. When he appeared at the Assizes, he was so starved and had suffered so much from cold and rain that his body was greatly swollen and his limbs were stiff, and he could not stand or walk. To take him to Scarborough Castle he was put on a horse, but was hardly able to keep his seat. At Scarborough, he had to spend fifty shillings to keep the rain and smoke out of his room; but as soon as he had been put to this expense, he was transferred to another room that had neither chimney nor fireplace. It faced the sea, and the wind drove the rain into the room; and when his clothes were wet through, he had no fire to dry them. His food consisted chiefly of bread and water: he had to buy the bread himself. What strange customs they had in those days, when prisoners had to pay for their food and for repairs to the prison! Many visitors came to see him and argue with him: doctors, magistrates, men of learning of various religions; but Friends were not admitted. After he had been in Scarborough more than a year he wrote a letter to the king, who ordered his release. The following day the Great Fire broke out in London; he said that he had had a presentiment of it during his imprisonment at Lancaster.

Finally, from 1673 to 1675, he underwent his last imprisonment, in Worcester and London, being falsely accused of breaking the Conventicle Act, which forbade unauthorized gatherings of more than four persons. As he was to appear before the Court of the King's Bench, he was sent to London. There he was set free upon his promising to appear before the next assize at Worcester. He fell ill there in prison and, one night while he was lying awake in bed 'in the glory of the Lord which was over all, it was said unto me that the Lord had a great deal more work

A Quaker's certificate of affirmation, made instead of taking the oath of allegiance (1723).

for me to do for him before he took me to himself'. Margaret Fox went to the king to ask for her husband's liberty, but, feeling he was guilty of nothing, Fox refused the royal pardon that was offered him and wished to be judged according to the law. After tiresome arguments in court, and eighteen months' imprisonment for no reason, he was released 'without receiving any pardon or coming under any obligation or engagement at all'. During his captivity at Worcester, in spite of his illness and although he was so often shuttlecocked between London and his prison, he wrote several books, and many papers and epistles to Friends 'to encourage and strengthen them in their services for God'.

The Toleration Act (1689) came only two years before the death of George Fox in London on 13 January 1691, in his sixty-seventh year, after a life well filled by the struggles he had had to wage, both to spread his principles and to defend them against his enemies without and within the movement.

In 1931 the *Church Times*, reviewing C. E. Whiting's *Studies in English Puritanism*, said, 'But the unfortunate Quakers deserve much sympathy, for their gentle persistence, in face of all trials, had a great deal to do with bringing into being religious liberty as we know it today.'

Countryfolk and courtiers.

George Fox and Social Injustice

Let us now see how awareness of the Inner Light affected social life, and the duties of man to man and class to class. Fox lived in a world where most of those who professed Christianity found it natural and inevitable that life should hinder the growth of the 'divine seed' in the hearts of men. His insight made him perceive injustices at once, and his loyalty to Christ made him denounce them boldly.

> How are you in the pure Religion, to visit the sick, the fatherless, and the widows, when both blind, and sick, and halt and lame lie up and down, cry up and down almost in every corner of the city, and men and women are so decked with gold and silver in their delicate state, that they cannot tell how to go. Surely, surely you know not that you are all of one mould and blood, that dwell upon the face of the earth. Would not a little out of your abundance and superfluity maintain these poor children, halt, lame, and blind, or set them at work that can work and they that cannot, find a place of relief for them; would not that be a grace to you?[1]

Thomas Ellwood, who afterwards read Latin to Milton, was attracted to Quakerism, and said that the vanity and useless

[1] *Doctrinals to Magistrates* (1657).

elegance of his clothes was revealed to him so sharply that he forthwith stripped off his lace, ribbons, and useless buttons, and gave up wearing rings.

The problem of poverty held the attention of Quakers from the beginning. In 1659, Fox recommended each meeting to take care of its poor, to provide work for those who were unemployed or were compelled for conscience' sake to give up their livelihood. Parents were to be helped to educate their children, so that there should be no beggars amongst Friends. In 1660, Fox wrote concerning Skipton General Meeting:

> . . . I was moved to set up that meeting, for many Friends suffered and their goods were spoiled wrongfully, contrary to the law. And so several Friends that had been justices and magistrates and that did understand the law came there and were able to inform Friends, and to gather up the sufferings that they might be laid before the justices and judges.
>
> And justices and captains had come to break up this meeting, but when they saw Friends' books and accounts of collections concerning the poor, how that we did take care one county to help another (and to provide for our poor that none of them should be chargeable to their parishes, etc.), and took care to help Friends beyond the seas, the justices and officers were made to confess that we did their work and Friends desired them to come and sit with them then.
>
> And so they passed away lovingly and commended Friends' practice.
>
> And many times there would be two hundred beggars of the world there, for all the country knew we met about the poor; wherefore after the meeting was done Friends would send to the bakers and give them each a penny loaf apiece, be they as many as they would; for we were taught to do good unto all but especially to the household of faith (p. 373).

In 1675, Meeting for Sufferings was established, to co-ordinate the help given to persecuted Friends all over the country.

At the beginning of his ministry, in 1648, we find Fox at Mansfield, only twenty-four years of age, exhorting the justices responsible for fixing servants' wages '. . . not to oppress the servants in their wages, but to do that which was right and just to them . . .'. At the same time, he asked the servants 'to do their duties, and serve honestly, etc.' In 1658 he wrote to Cromwell and Parliament, asking that begging should be suppressed, saying that it was need that made people steal, and that those who were rich must provide work for the poor. About the same time he demanded the closing of superfluous inns and taverns, and he wrote to 'such as kept public-houses for entertainment, that they should not let people have more drink than would do them good'. When he was in Cornwall in 1659, he noticed that the population set out to cause shipwrecks, so as to get as much of the wreck as they could; he wrote a long letter to all the parishes to reprove them for such inhuman actions.[1]

While he was in prison at Derby he saw the injustices of the judicial system, and he wrote to the judges: '. . . concerning their putting men to death for cattle and for money and small things. . . . And I also writ . . . what a sore thing it was that prisoners should lie so long in gaol, and how that they learned badness one of another in talking of their bad deeds, and therefore speedy justice should have been done' (pp. 65, 66).

In 1669 Fox demanded the opening of 'an alms-house or hospital for all poor Friends, that are past work', but this wish could not be fulfilled until some years after his death. Having noticed the cruel treatment inflicted on the insane, he recommended, in that same year 1669, 'a house for them that be distempered', thus showing, two hundred years before his time, the need for treating insanity as an illness.

As for negro slavery, we have already seen that he exhorted their owners to treat the blacks 'mildly and gently . . . and not use cruelty towards them, as the manner of some hath been and is, and to make them free after thirty years servitude'. He also said that the situation of the slave should be looked upon as a great captivity and a great cruelty. Unlike the white population of the time, Fox thought that the Light of God was in slaves' souls, too, at least in a certain measure. As is well known, it was

[1] See Grubb, op. cit., p. 158.

not until 1776 that the Quakers of Philadelphia decided to exclude from the Society of Friends those who persisted in holding slaves. We shall come back to that subject. We have also seen that Fox gave women their due place in society, by allowing them to speak in meetings for worship. In 1658 he summoned to London sixty women Friends to form a group that should come to the aid of Quakers who were poor, sick, or in prison, as well as of widows and orphans.

The problem of education was not forgotten. He founded a girls' school at Shacklewell in London, so as to instruct them 'in whatsoever things were civil and useful in the creation'. (It should be remembered that the famous French boarding-school for girls at St. Cyr, founded by Mme de Maintenon and Louis XIV in 1685, came fifteen years later.) In 1669 Fox asked for a school to be opened for children at Waltham in Hertfordshire. In 1670 both these schools were in full operation, and they became extremely prosperous for a time. Another Friend, Thomas Lawson, a distinguished schoolmaster and botanist, in 1660 addressed *An Appeal to the Parliament, concerning the Poor, that there may not be a Beggar in England.* He proposed that a 'poor man's office' or labour bureau should be set up in each parish, putting employers in touch with workmen, future apprentices, and servants. But, he added, no girls should be 'put to service until they first be taught to spin, knit, sew, or learn some trade or way of livelihood'.[1]

Among the Quaker personalities who were George Fox's contemporaries we must mention John Bellers, born in 1654, who may be considered the pioneer of modern Christian socialism. He published numerous schemes which made Karl Marx say in years to come that he was 'a veritable phenomenon in the history of political economy'.[2] Bellers' ideas, a century in advance of their time, are set forth in his work *Proposals for raising a College of Industry.* He stated that the prosperity of a country could only be maintained if the industrial and agricultural classes increased their output, and if high wages were paid to workers.

[1] Quoted in *Second Period of Quakerism*, by W. C. Braithwaite.
[2] *Das Kapital*, 2nd edn., vol. i, p. 515.

'The increase of regular labouring people is the kingdom's greatest treasure, strength and honour.'

His College of Industry proposed a sort of community composed of about 300 poor people—men, women, and children—plying every kind of trade. With an initial capital of about £18,000, land was to be bought and buildings erected. The money was to come from the subscriptions of the rich: 'a comfortable living in the college to the industrious labourer being the rich man's debt and not their charity to them; labour giving the labourer as good a right to a living there as the rich men's estates do them'. Old people and those who were ill would receive the necessary care, and children a liberal education. Each community would have its library; and libraries could hardly be found anywhere at that time. That is, in outline, his remarkable project; reading the text of it, one finds it hard to imagine that it was published as early as 1695. He intended that these colleges should be founded all over the country, but the only practical fruit of his suggestions was the leasing, by London and Middlesex Quarterly Meeting, of a workhouse at Clerkenwell in London. This community has lasted unbroken to the present day: it is now known as the Friends' School, Saffron Walden. A National Health Service was also in Bellers' mind, with his demand for free dispensaries and for hospitals; and he wanted each parish to pay its own doctors. He protested against the death penalty, which struck at men and women and even children guilty of minor crimes. He denounced the frightful state of the prisons, and tried to reform the electoral system for parliamentary elections. Finally, like William Penn, he wrote down his dreams of a federation of European states. Karl Marx, writing in German in the nineteenth century, at last gave Bellers his due: he is now better-known in the Soviet Union than in England.

Right from the start, the new Society based its conduct on the most scrupulous honesty. Many people 'of the world' were shocked at Friends' setting fixed prices on their goods instead of following the custom of bargaining, as well as at their plain speech and manners. In the *Journal*, Fox tells how 'many

Friends, being tradesmen of several sorts lost their custom at the first; for the people would not trade with them nor trust them, and for a time Friends that were tradesmen could hardly get enough money to buy bread. But afterwards people came to see Friends' honesty and truthfulness and "yea" and "nay" at a word in their dealing, and their lives and conversations did preach and reach to the witness of God in all people, and they knew and saw that, for conscience sake towards God, they would not cozen and cheat them, and at last that they might send any child and be as well used as themselves, at any of their shops' (p. 169). It has often been said that England owes to Quaker example the introduction of fixed prices in retail trading.

The Quaker contribution to social life has been summed up as follows:

1. The treatment of all life as a sacred thing, thus making social service a sacred duty.
2. Sensitiveness to oppression and injustice, due to the habit of following the light.
3. A sincerity of behaviour, which, in courts of justice, refused oaths, in civil life rejected all servilities and flattering titles and compelled simplicity of dress and address, and, in business, obliged men to plain and straightforward dealing, at fixed prices.
4. An inwardly controlled temperance, which retrenched luxuries, frivolities and excesses in food or drink, as pampering the lower self and contrary to the service of God.
5. A Puritan outlook on art and recreations.
6. A recognition of the Divine worth of every human being, which overthrew the dominance of racial and class distinctions and gave woman her place of equal comradeship with man.[1]

[1] W. C. Braithwaite, *The Beginnings of Quakerism*, p. 556.

Der Große betrieger und Falsche MESSIAS
IACOB NAYLOR
König der Quacker
ANNO 1657.

A German caricature: 'The Great deceiver and False MESSIAH JAMES
NAYLOR, *King of the Quakers in the Year 1657.' The small picture inset
shows the first part of Nayler's punishment, when he rode through Bristol facing
backwards, to be whipped in the market-place.*

James Nayler:
Private *versus* Corporate Judgement

It is not surprising that the wave of enthusiasm that had carried forward the preaching of George Fox and his early collaborators also bore with it a certain number of fanatical or even unbalanced minds. However, the extravagances of the early years became rarer as the movement gathered strength. The most serious trouble occurred in 1656, when Fox had just been released from the dungeon at Launceston. He had to face a far more serious difficulty than those caused by the unimportant stupidities of a few excited Friends. One of his best, sincerest, and most pious fellow-workers, James Nayler, had suffered untold privations, ill-treatment, lengthy imprisonment, and overwork, and he had a nervous breakdown: he completely lost his head over the enthusiasm he was being greeted with, particularly by women.

He was persuaded to leave London and visit Fox in Launceston gaol, but was arrested on the way and imprisoned at Exeter. Fox went to see him in prison in the hope of persuading him that he was making a shocking mistake. Nayler was stubborn.

> The next day [writes Fox] I spake to James Nayler again: and he slighted what I said and was dark and much out; yet he would have come and kissed me. But I said that since he had turned against the power of God, I could not receive his show of kindness; the Lord moved me to slight him, and to set the power of God over him. So after I had been warring with the world, there was now a wicked spirit risen up amongst Friends to war against.[1]

When released, Nayler with his followers rode north. Entering Bristol in the rain, with his half-dozen admirers shouting 'Holy, holy, holy!' and casting down their garments before his horse, Nayler may have forgotten that he had in his pocket a

[1] *Journal* (Everyman's Library edn., 1924), p. 137.

James Nailor Quaker, set 2 howers on the Pillory at Westminster whiped by the Hang
man to the old Exchainge London, Som daves after, Stood too howers more on the Pillory
yt at the Exchainge, and there had his Tongue Bored throug with a hot Iron, &
Stigmatized in the Forehead with the Letter:B: Decemt: 17 anno Domi:1656:

Nayler's punishment.

letter ending with the fatal words 'Thy name shall be no more
James Nayler but Jesus.'[1] Arrested and searched, Nayler was
found guilty of 'horrid blasphemy'. He was condemned to the
pillory and was whipped through the streets of London. He had
his tongue bored with a hot iron, was branded on his forehead
with the letter B, and was condemned to be imprisoned till the
pleasure of Parliament should be known. During the three
years he spent in prison, he became aware of his errors; he made
a public apology when he came out again, and published a long
confession in which he humbly admitted his past mistakes. He
was reconciled with George Fox in 1660, some months before his
death at the age of forty-four. He had set out for Yorkshire to
see his family, when he was attacked by highwaymen. Here are
the words he uttered two hours before he died:

> There is a spirit which I feel that delights to do no evil, nor to
> revenge any wrong, but delights to endure all things, in hope to
> enjoy its own in the end. Its hope is to outlive all wrath and con-

[1] See Nayler's Works, 1716, pp. lii, liii.

74

*One of Nayler's writings, re-published after his death.
The long-winded title is characteristic of the time.*

tention, and to weary out all exaltation and cruelty, or whatever is of a nature contrary to itself. It sees to the end of all temptations. As it bears no evil in itself, so it conceives none in thoughts to any other. If it be betrayed, it bears it, for its ground and spring is the mercies and forgiveness of God. Its crown is meekness, its life is everlasting love unfeigned; it takes its kingdom with entreaty and not with contention, and keeps it by lowliness of mind. In God alone it can rejoice, though none else regard it, or can own its life. It's conceived in sorrow, and brought forth without any to pity it, nor doth it murmur at grief and oppression. It never rejoiceth but through sufferings: for with the world's joy it is murdered. I found it alone, being forsaken. I have fellowship therein with them who through death obtained this resurrection and eternal holy life.

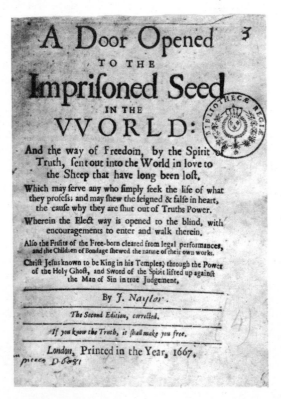

A Door Opened

TO THE

Imprisoned Seed

IN THE

VVORLD:

And the way of Freedom, by the Spirit of Truth, sent out into the World in love to the Sheep that have long been lost,

Which may serve any who simply seek the life of what they profess; and may shew the feigned & false in heart, the cause why they are shut out of Truths Power.

Wherein the Elect way is opened to the blind, with encouragements to enter and walk therein.

Also the Fruits of the Free-born cleared from legal performances, and the Children of Bondage shewed the nature of their own works.

Christ Jesus known to be King in his Temples, through the Power of the Holy Ghost, and Sword of the Spirit lifted up against the Man of Sin in true Judgement,

By *J. Naylor*.

The Second Edition, corrected.

If you know the Truth, it shall make you free.

London, Printed in the Year, 1667.

Thou wast with me when I fled from the face of mine enemies: then Thou didst warn me in the night: Thou carriedst me in Thy power into the hiding-place Thou hadst prepared for me; there Thou covered me with Thy hand, that in time thou mightst bring me forth a rock before all the world. When I was weak Thou stayedst me with Thy hand, that in Thy time Thou mightst present me to the world in strength in which I stand, and cannot be moved. Praise the Lord, O my soul. Let this be written for those that come after. Praise the Lord.[1]

Few are the words of man that can be compared with those, as the expression of a soul that has found peace at the last.

The aberration of Nayler and some of his followers deeply affected Fox and his friends. There is no doubt that these actions had a real influence on the direction in which the Society was moving. With the passing of years it can indeed be seen that although Fox was still sure of the witness he was bearing to the Inner Light in the heart of all men, he felt no less keenly that members of the Society of Friends needed to express their opinions collectively. Individual freedom would have become sheer anarchy among excited people, or with pathological subjects like James Nayler. Six years after Nayler's death, and as a result of some quite unimportant difficulties, 'a group of leading Friends issued a letter asserting the authority of a meeting to exclude from its fellowship persons who persisted in rejecting its judgement. . . . This letter, by definitely subordinating individual guidance to the sense of the meeting as a whole, marked an important step in Quaker development.'[2]

[1] Edmund Rubbra has composed a beautiful setting of these words for soprano solo and chorus. For a discussion of how these words have come down to us, see the article by Ormerod Greenwood in the *Journal of the Friends' Historical Society*, Spring 1958 (Vol. 48, No. 5, p. 199).

[2] Howard Brinton, *Friends for 300 Years* (London, 1952), p. 101.

Organization

The doctrine of the Inner Light, as Fox understood it, did not do away with corporate authority. It did profoundly affect the character of that authority, particularly the manner in which it was exercised. To begin with, authority is lodged in the whole community, and not in any class within the community. The maintenance of discipline rests primarily with the local meeting, subject to a successive appeal to the monthly, quarterly, and yearly meetings. Each of these represents a larger area, and the yearly meetings, which have been held in unbroken succession since 1668, represent the whole country. In the method of arriving at decisions, respect for that of God in the individual is fundamental. Every individual member is responsible for the maintenance of discipline and the exercise of authority just as every member is responsible for the ministry. Discussion of practical issues must therefore be free and open. It must also be conducted in a spirit of waiting upon God. There must be no striving for victory, nothing but seeking for Truth.[1]

Any religious society which wants to endure must necessarily rely on some form of organization; but in the early days there was no such thing among the Children of the Light, Fox's first followers. We have already seen that he had no desire to found a new Church. As T. Edmund Harvey said in *The Rise of the Quakers*: 'George Fox had probably no more idea of founding a new sect than had Luther of separating Christendom into two great divisions of Protestant and Catholic. Their object was to set forth anew the living Gospel, to draw men to it and away from shams, to proclaim a great and universal message, not to organize a party or create a new association of people.'

The persecutions that came upon them, from the beginning of Fox's ministry, hastened the inevitable movement towards cohesion and association. Help had to be given to Friends in prison and to their families. Meeting for Sufferings was founded

[1] H. G. Wood, *George Fox* (1912), p. 118.

for this purpose in 1675; itinerant missionaries had to be supported; and the Society had to meet the needs of its living, growing, corporate life, confident of the truth it treasured.

A spiritual movement, as it takes shape in organized form, has one fatal danger to meet; it may crystallize and gradually replace the Spirit by the conservative organization. The early Friends saw this danger ahead, as Fox later saw the danger of anarchy; a certain equilibrium had to be found between these opposing tendencies, natural enough amongst human beings. This was the point at which Fox's genius was revealed, for the organization he chiefly inspired has remained virtually unaltered in all countries for the best part of three hundred years.

As early as 1652, William Dewsbury, one of Fox's very first followers, was asking for the organization of general meetings to examine urgent problems. His demands were published as 'the word of the living God to His Church'. Other leaders spoke in similar terms and with the same prophetic authority; yet they were very careful not to lay down a code of rules and regulations. In 1656, at the conclusion of a meeting of Elders at Balby in Yorkshire, a letter on twenty points of conduct was sent 'from the Spirit of Truth to the Children of the Light', giving counsel rather than drawing up rules. The letter ends thus: 'Dearly beloved friends, these things we do not lay upon you as a rule or form to walk by, but that all with the measure of light which is pure and holy may be guided, and so in the light walking and abiding these may be fulfilled in the spirit, not from the letter; for the letter killeth, but the spirit giveth life.'[1]

The first business meeting seems to have been established in 1654. Subsequent meetings were local and monthly. The first General Meeting took place in 1658. London Yearly Meeting has been held annually since 1668. Yearly Meetings were gradually set up in other countries, particularly in Ireland and North America.

The unit in the organization is the Particular Meeting, comprising all the members living within the compass of a place of worship. Representatives of the local Meeting join with others

[1] This paragraph closely follows Brinton, op. cit., pp. 99–100.

from neighbouring Meetings once a month for worship and the transaction of business in Monthly Meetings. Further, Monthly Meetings of a larger area send their representatives four times a year to Quarterly Meetings; and finally there is the Yearly Meeting. All these meetings are open not only to the appointed representatives, but also to any member of the Society who wishes to take part. Meeting for Sufferings, which first met in 1675, still keeps its name in England; it is in fact the executive committee for all business arising between one Yearly Meeting and the next. As we have said, there have been hardly any modifications in the organization set up by Fox, particularly since his liberation from Scarborough (1665–6), when he seems to have felt the

The movement was given uniformity in the 18th century by intervisitation of meetings, almost as though the Atlantic Ocean were no obstacle. This map, copied by S. Bradford (1740) shows distances in miles from Sutton Benger (near Chippenham, Wilts.) to other Friends' meetings.

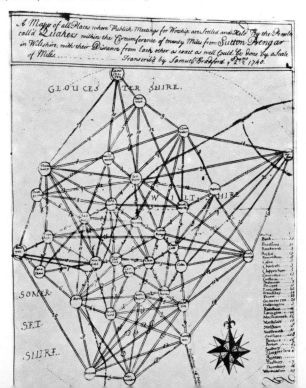

A Table of Heads

urgent need to organize meetings in each county, modelled on what had been done in the north of England. This same organization engaged his full attention during his journeys in the American colonies.

In his introduction to the Everyman edition of Fox's *Journal*, Professor Rufus M. Jones wrote:

> The type of organisation which Fox developed for the groups of followers gathered around him indicates plainly enough that he was not a lonely dreamer but a practical leader of men, though here, again, he did not absolutely *originate* something wholly new and unique. He saw the latent possibilities in the simple types of group-fellowship that already existed and he expanded these and worked them out into new and fresh ways of expression. . . . It was marked by almost utter simplicity of structure and method. There were no essential officials, no ritual, no programme, no outward and visible sacraments, no music, no paraphernalia of any kind. . . . There was the widest freedom and the greatest possible stretch of the principle of democracy. One might have supposed that chaos would have resulted, but it did not result. . . . For almost three centuries this group-fellowship and this gentle, unauthoritative leadership have weathered the storms and the stress and the strain of the years.

At the death of Fox, in 1691, in spite of the most frightful persecution, there were about 50,000 Quakers in England and Ireland, out of a population of about five million. There were also groups in Holland, New England, Pennsylvania, Maryland, Virginia, and the Carolinas.

The Monthly Meeting is most important; it has many duties: it deals with candidates for membership and with resignations; is concerned with the education of children and with births, marriages, and deaths; appoints Elders (responsible mainly for the right holding of meetings for worship) and Overseers (responsible mainly for pastoral care and giving guidance in practical matters). It used to appoint Ministers as well, amongst those recognized as being particularly gifted in the spoken ministry; but this custom ceased in England after the first World War. More than ever the responsibility for the spoken word

Index to Christian and Brotherly Advices Given Forth from Time to Time by Yearly Meeting in London; alphabetically digested under proper Heads. (1738). *All Monthly Meetings received a copy of this manuscript volume, bound in green vellum.*

rests upon each one present at a meeting for worship, in virtue of the 'priesthood of all believers'.

From the early days of the movement, Friends were very careful to record births and deaths for their members; but the question of marriage was more delicate. They refused to recognize that any 'priest' had the power to declare that two people were henceforth husband and wife. This is what Fox said at a wedding in 1666:

> In the meeting before the marriage I was moved to open to the people the state of our marriages, how the people of God took one another in the assemblies of the elders, and how God did join man and woman together before the Fall. And man had joined in the Fall but it was God's joining again in the restoration, and never from Genesis to the Revelation did ever any priests marry any (*Journal*, p. 506).

At that time a Quaker wedding was not legal, and Friends had had a great deal to endure because of this until 1661, when it was recognized by the law. At a meeting for worship for solemnizing a marriage, the custom was, and still is, that after a period of silent worship, the parties stand, and, taking each other by the hand, make in turn a short declaration by which they promise publicly to be faithful and loving to each other; the meeting for worship then continues. Fox recommended that there should be at least twelve members to witness a marriage ceremony. A certificate is signed by the parties and by all those present. The Society of Friends has always been careful to give young people a serious idea of marriage. It is well known that divorces in the Society are rare.[1]

When a member dies, it is usual to hold a special meeting for worship in memory of the deceased; anyone can of course pray or speak about him. The greatest simplicity has always been enjoined upon the Society in both funerals and tombstones, so that no distinction may be made between rich and poor. It is a Quaker tradition not to wear mourning, though nothing is laid down on this subject.

Collective leadership, as it should be among Friends, is safe-

[1] See Grubb, op. cit., p. 115.

A Quaker Wedding in 1820, by Percy Bigland (1896). The costumes are of 1820; the faces are of Friends alive in the 1890s: the small boy is George Gillett Whitney, until recently head of the art department at Westtown School, Pennsylvania.

guarded firstly by the religious spirit in which they are accustomed to meet, whether for worship or business, and secondly by the fact that they have never taken a vote at their meetings. 'So Friends are not to meet like a company of people about town or parish business,' wrote George Fox, 'but to wait upon the Lord; and feeling his Power, and Spirit to lead them, and order them to his glory' (*Epistles*, p. 349). If there are officials to be appointed, or candidates for membership to be interviewed, the meeting appoints a small committee to discuss and inquire; their recommendations are discussed at the following meeting. Applications for membership are never taken quickly or lightly. Business meetings are presided over by the Clerk, who combines the functions of chairman and secretary. He has to weigh up the sense of the meeting and express it in a minute, which he reads out there and then; if the minute is not acceptable to the meeting, the Clerk makes the necessary alterations to his draft, or discussion proceeds, or the matter is left to be discussed again at a later meeting. Where there is disagreement or confusion, it is not unusual for someone to suggest that the meeting may continue in silence for a few minutes; this often helps the meeting to reach a deeper, clearer understanding and a common agreement; in any case, it lowers the temperature, and checks any tendency for a member to rush to speak, when he should be pondering what has just been said. This method of doing business seeks to avoid hurting anyone in reaching a decision.

'Some problems', said Howard Brinton,[1] 'have been postponed for more than a century awaiting unity. Had a vote been taken as early as 1700 slavery would probably have been voted out, but a substantial minority would not have concurred. The subject was brought up again and again, progress was made slowly until in 1776 the Society was united in refusing membership to persons who held slaves.'

[1] Op. cit., p. 107.

William Penn, on top of the City Hall at Philadelphia.

The Quakers in America—
William Penn and the 'Holy Experiment'

In the colonies on the western side of the Atlantic, the Quakers found favourable opportunities for taking part in public life and making their influence felt. Before the first missionaries of the Society of Friends arrived, there were in New England many people who were longing for a truer religion than that of the established Churches. There, too, were Seekers blazing the trail for Quakerism and arousing the intolerance of the orthodox. Starting in 1653, many pamphlets were published against the Quakers; they were even accused of witchcraft. The Quakers failed to understand the Puritans, and the Puritans returned the compliment: they represented two very different types of reli-

85

gion. Harvard College had been founded to supply the Church with ministers expert in theology, whilst the Quakers had disparaged Oxford and Cambridge and admitted women to the ministry. The Puritan ministers, as paid professionals, were odious to the Quakers, who went so far as to call them 'black priests', 'priests of Baal', 'hireling ministers', etc., and received in return the epithets 'false prophets', 'seducers', 'antichrists' from the clergy. This clash, which in England remained a matter of heated argument, was growing far sharper in New England. There, Church and State being one, the Non-conformists were coming to be treated as public enemies and sedition-mongers. The struggle was going to be a fierce one.

As we have said above, the first fields of activity that opened to missionary work were the American colonies. A base of operations was set up in Barbados, from which Friends set out for the American continent. Persecution was fierce: they were expelled from Boston, and they were threatened with death if they returned to Massachusetts; but they returned. Four of them were executed at Boston between 1659 and 1661; one of these, Mary Dyer, who had been pardoned the previous year, was hanged because she had come back a third time. A few years previously, in 1656, two other women, Mary Fisher and Ann Austin, had come to Boston. They were arrested on board ship, their books were publicly burnt, and they were imprisoned for five weeks, and sent back to Barbados. A couple of days later, eight more Friends arrived from England. They were imprisoned, and then shipped back to England. A year later, another woman, Mary Clark, left her husband and her six children, to come and testify to the inhabitants of Boston after a long and difficult voyage. She was arrested in the street as she was delivering her message, condemned to receive upon her bare back twenty lashes of a three-cord whip, and was thrown into prison for three months. After that she was banished. By order of Governor Endicott, some who disobeyed the religious laws were starved; others had their ears cut off or their tongues bored through with a red-hot iron. Anyone suspected of belonging to the Quaker movement was condemned to death or banished.

Mary Dyer, on her way to the gallows in Boston, Mass., in 1660. A modern imaginative drawing.

In spite of four laws passed against the Quakers in 1656–8, Quakerism continued to grow. The death penalty mentioned above was abandoned in 1661, after an impish intervention by Charles II: in response to an appeal from Friends, he agreed to send a banned Quaker, Thomas Shattuck, back to Boston to carry the royal order stopping the executions. Governor Endicott had to eat humble pie and remove his own hat before the king's messenger. But Friends had to go on striving for another twenty years before persecution ceased and the law banishing Quakers was repealed. In the other colonies of Rhode Island, New Jersey, North and South Carolina, the situation was very different, and among the Friends were many administrators and even Governors. Amelia M. Gummere, writing on *The Early*

87

HOMANNO MAP OF 1687

Quakers in New Jersey, says, 'Their staunch integrity and courageous defence of their actions in everything that involved a sense of duty to the public, is beyond praise, and undoubtedly was an important factor in forming the government of the state upon present lines.'[1]

Before studying the history of Pennsylvania and its founder, William Penn, let us sum up[2] the situation of the Quakers in North America by saying that the Golden Age of Quakerism in that part of the world came between about 1700 and 1740. Pennsylvania had a Quaker assembly and its capital, Philadelphia, was the cultural centre of the New World. In Rhode Island, half the population was Quaker and for thirty-six terms —for more than a century—the colony had a Quaker Governor. On one occasion the Governor and half the representatives in the state parliament of North Carolina were Quakers. New Jersey was owned by Friends; and long after giving up their rights in 1702 they had a strong influence in the government of the province. In the Quaker towns, the Meeting was the spiritual, intellectual, and economic centre. Any disagreements were settled there, in the group's customary meetings. A library and

[1] Quoted by Grubb, op. cit., p. 144, from R. M. Jones, *The Quakers in the American Colonies*, p. 385.

[2] See Grubb, op. cit., pp. 146, 142.

A new meeting-house in North Carolina in 1791.

◄ *A map dated 1687 already showed Philadelphia; it was published in Germany by Homanno of Nuremberg.*

One of several versions of Penn in armour at the age of 22. It is not at present certain when or where the original portrait was painted.

a school were part of its organization. The poor were helped, and marriages approved and celebrated. Police forces were kept to a minimum. This flowering of Quakerism was not distinguished by anything remarkable in the way of literature or art; what mattered most was the life of the home, the Meeting, and the community. At the end of the eighteenth century, there were about sixty schools in Pennsylvania and about thirty in New Jersey.

William Penn[1] is the best-known of the Quakers, and the founder of Pennsylvania. He was born in London, on Tower Hill, on 16 October 1644, the son of Admiral Penn, and descended from a very old family in the south of England. The grandfather had been something of a freebooter, trading from

[1] Some of the details of this account of Penn are drawn from Bonamy Dobrée, *William Penn, Quaker and Pioneer* (Constable, London, 1932).

the northern seas to Spain and Morocco; the father, a go-getter, became a sea-captain at twenty, supported Cromwell, and was promoted vice-admiral at twenty-five. He was an ambitious courtier, though not so black as Pepys has painted him. How William Penn became a saintly man and one of the greatest statesmen in history with that inheritance is a mystery. God's grace and his choosing are unfathomable.

Returning from the expedition that took Jamaica but failed to capture Spanish treasure at Hispaniola, the admiral was arrested and had to retire. In 1660, he carried to Breda in Holland the invitation from Parliament asking the exiled Charles II to return as king. Charles knighted him, promoted him Admiral of Ireland, and gave him a house in London. The son, aged sixteen, was sent up to Oxford to study. Oxford University had become a theological battleground. The undergraduates were divided into two hostile camps, the conformists or Anglicans on one side, and the Non-conformists on the other. Young Penn promptly sided with the Non-conformists—the Puritans. He was strongly against the social customs prevailing, and was attracted by the republican ideas of the Puritans. He was well read in history and theology, spoke several modern languages, and was an accomplished sportsman. He became a leading personality amongst the undergraduates. He was soon being fined for non-attendance at his college chapel; his resistance to authority was strengthened by his visits to the Puritan Dr. Owen, who had lost his University post at the Restoration and was living outside the city. Penn was deeply disturbed at the way of life of many of his fellow-students: 'hellish darkness and debauchery', he called it; and he was probably involved in a free fight between groups of students, as well as falling foul of the college authorities by what he had written. Early in 1661 he was sent down: it was a terrible blow for a father who had a well-founded ambition that his son might one day be an ambassador.

The admiral sent his son to Paris, to broaden his experience of the world and take his mind off religion. The Court of Louis XIV, who was a young man of enormous vitality, was then a place of dazzling brilliance. Penn did not stay long in

Paris, but went on to Saumur for two years, where he studied at the Huguenot Academy under Moyse Amyraut, who for thirty years had been a famous protagonist of toleration. Protestant theological students went there from all over Europe, and prominent English families sent their sons to him to learn French in a sheltered environment. Amyraut died in 1664, so Penn went on to Italy, but was summoned home by his father because a Dutch war was threatening. He came back a fashionable young man, and created a good impression in London with his French pantaloons: Mrs. Pepys thought him 'a most modish person, grown . . . a fine gentleman'. His father made him study law at Lincoln's Inn; his studies were interrupted by service with the navy, in the 1665 campaign against the Dutch. As the summer of that year drew on, the Great Plague cast its mounting terror over London, and the Penns, unlike most of the upper-class families, stayed on at their work; the son naturally became solemn and sad again. The next year his father sent him to Ireland. He fought with distinction in helping to put down a mutiny, and thought of taking up arms as his career; the well-known portrait *Penn in Armour* evokes this stage in his life. However, his father set him to manage the family estate. Quakerism seemed a long way away; yet it was in Ireland that, as a boy of fourteen, he had seen his father and his father's negro manservant in tears at the preaching of the young Quaker, Thomas Loe; that God could speak directly within the hearts of men was true for the boy too, as he had already experienced it a couple of years previously. The first meeting with Thomas Loe had occurred at the family castle in County Cork; and it was at Cork in 1667 that Penn seized with enthusiasm on a second opportunity of hearing Thomas Loe. 'There is a faith which overcomes the world, and there is a faith which is overcome by the world', he began. Penn was convinced. He threw in his lot with the Quakers. At a second meeting, interrupted by a noisy soldier whom Penn ejected, he and other Friends were arrested. What a disgrace for the admiral! Before long the story leaked out. 'Son William,' he wrote, '. . . I charge you and strictly command you that you come to me with all possible

The garret in the Governor's House in the Tower of London where Penn wrote No Cross No Crown.

NO
Cross, no Crovvn:

Or several Sober
REASONS

Against

Hat-Honour, Titular-Respects, You to a
single Person, with the *Apparel* and
Recreations of the Times:

Being inconsistant with Scripture, Reason, and the
Practice, as well of the best Heathens, as the holy Men
and Women of all Generations; and consequently
fantastick, impertinent and sinfull.

With Sixty Eight Testimonies of the most famous Persons,
of both former and latter Ages for further confirmation.

In Defence of the poor despised *Quakers*, against
the Practice and Objections of their Adversaries.

By W. Penn *jᵒ*
*An humble Disciple, and patient Bearer of the
Cross of Jesus.*

But Mordecai bowed not, Esth. 3. 2. Adam where art thou? Gen. 3. 9.
In like manner the women adorn themselves in modest Apparel, not
with broidered hair, &c. 1 Tim. 2. 9. Thy Law is my Meditation all
the day, Psal. 119. 97.

Printed in the Year, 1669.

No Cross, No Crown (1669).

speed. In expectation of your compliance, I remain, Your affectionate father, W. Penn.' Son William returned without haste, visiting meetings on the way. There was an amazing scene when the father, locking the door of the room in which he was interviewing his son, solemnly announced that he was going to pray to Almighty God that his son might never go to a Quaker meeting again. William, aghast at the blasphemy, threatened to jump out of the window. A chance visitor saved the situation by calling to congratulate the admiral on his son's strength of character!

Penn was later turned out of the house, and worked with Friends. The famous story of the sword is apocryphal, but true to the character of the men concerned: George Fox, asked by Penn if he should cease wearing his sword, replied 'Wear it as long as thou canst.' He soon left it off.

He launched into controversy: *Truth Exalted* was his first pamphlet; a second answered attacks on Quakerism; a third, *The Sandy Foundation Shaken*, which he aimed at a seedy minister named Vincent, appeared to attack the doctrine of the Trinity. This shocked the authorities, and Penn spent the next seven months in the Tower of London. It was hoped that the imprisonment would make the young man give way, but peace was in his soul. The Bishop of London had said Penn should retract, or die in prison. Penn flung back a dignified answer: 'All is well; I wish they had told me so before, since the expecting of a release put a stop to some business; thou may'st tell my father, who I know will ask thee, these words; that my prison shall be my grave before I will budge a jot; for I owe my conscience to no mortal man; I have no need to fear, God will make amends for all.'

The months passed. Penn, in his solitude, wrote his greatest work, *No Cross, No Crown*, which is one of the classics of the English language. He marshals his arguments as a chess-player his pawns and pieces; his father, however, will not have been pleased to read such gems as: 'To be descended of wealth or titles, fills no man's head with brains, or heart with truth; those qualities come from an higher source.' The second part of the book is devoted to the testimonies—the Famous Last Words, to use a modern catch-phrase—of sixty-eight eminent persons, ancient and modern; done entirely from memory, this was a *tour de force*. (In the second edition, he quoted the testimonies of forty-six kings, emperors, and Greek or Roman rulers, thirty-two pagan philosophers, eleven virtuous women, twenty-five apostles and fathers of the Church, and finally thirty-nine great persons of modern times.) Still in prison, Penn wrote a much shorter work, *Innocency with her Open Face*, to explain and justify *The Sandy Foundation Shaken*; he had already resisted the appeals of his father and of the gracious Dr. Stillingfleet. He had charged the latter with a message to the king, 'that the Tower was the worst argument in the world to convince me; for whoever was in the wrong, those who used force for religion could never be in the right'.

His unflinching conduct, his pamphlet, a letter to the Secretary of State, Lord Arlington, and possibly his father's influence, procured his release in July 1669. He had won. A year after his return home, he went as was expected to a Sunday morning meeting in Gracechurch Street. The doors were locked and guarded. Meeting was therefore held in the street. Penn removed his hat and began to preach. 'There were some watchmen with halberds and musketeers came to take him down while he was speaking; but the multitude crowded so close about him that they could not come to him; but, to prevent further disturbance, he promised when the meeting was done to come to them.' Thus wrote a fellow-worshipper, John Rous. Penn and William Meade were arrested on a warrant, previously prepared, charging them with riot (which entitled them to be tried by jury). Penn wrote a tactful letter to his father from his prison lodging at the Black Dog in Newgate market, pointing out that members of other denominations were being arrested too; the Conventicle Act had been revived. The trial at the Old Bailey a fortnight later is one of the most important ever staged in England. Penn and his companion were accused of preaching and being present at a meeting which caused a riot. Under what law were they indicted? asked Penn. Under the common law, the Recorder answered, but was unable to define it further. If it was so hard to understand, it could not be common, retorted Penn. *Recorder*: 'Sir, you are a troublesome fellow, and it is not for the honour of the court to suffer you to go on.' *Penn*: 'I have asked but one question, and you have not answered me; though the rights and privileges of every Englishman be concerned in it.'

And so the argument continued, with Penn's wonderful courage and his clear understanding of the law winning the jury over to his side. After an hour and a half's retirement, the jury came back, and their foreman, Edward Bushell, announced that they found Penn guilty—of speaking in Gracechurch Street (which was not an offence). Sent out, they repeated it in writing half an hour later. They were locked up in a bare room over-

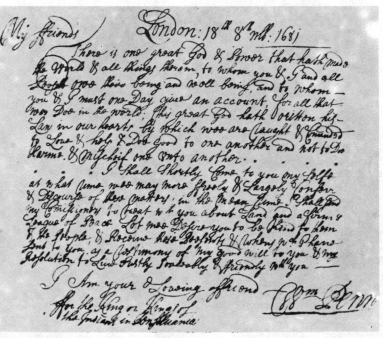

Letter from William Penn 'for the King or Kings of the Indians': 'My Friends, There is one great God and Power that hath made the World . . .'

night, without food or water. At the following sitting, on Sunday morning, they stuck to their verdict; Penn reminded the judges of Magna Carta; and the bench fumed and raged. On Monday, the jury, their verdict still not being accepted, altered it to Not Guilty. However, the jury were kept in prison for a couple of months and two years later they had finally won their case (known as Bushell's Case), establishing the rights and privileges of the English jury. Penn and his companion, however, had had their fines secretly paid by the dying admiral, who dearly wished to see his son again.

Penn travelled to Holland and Germany in 1670, and again in 1677—this time with George Fox and Robert Barclay (see p. 55). In 1672, at the age of twenty-eight, he married Guli Springett, stepdaughter of Isaac Penington, 'the love of my youth and much the joy of my life'. He poured out his abundant energy in pamphlets, letters, theological disputations with cranks and others, and in visiting Meetings with his wife. He was accused of being a Jesuit in disguise, because he claimed liberty of conscience for all, even for Catholics.

But the more he fought, the more he realized that it was almost impossible to obtain such liberty. He began to dream again of a wonderful land where every man might worship God according to his lights. His attention was drawn to New Jersey, in North America, by two Quakers who had taken refuge there and who had consulted him about the allocation of land. Penn became filled with enthusiasm for their ideas, and drafted a constitution, the main features of which were freedom of worship, universal suffrage, and the sovereignty of the people.

The Crown of England owed William Penn the sum of about £16,000, which Charles II, perpetually short of money, had no hope of repaying in cash. Penn asked to be paid in land, so that he could found the colony of his dreams. The Crown made over to him lands north of Maryland, with a magnificent site for a harbour on the estuary of the Delaware river. The land was covered with dense forests and inhabited by Red Indians. Penn published his plan as a letter, adding a description of the country. He christened this project 'The Holy Experiment'.

The Treaty between Penn and the Indians 1683: a version of the painting by Benjamin West (1738–1820), one-time President of the Royal Academy. The Indian costumes are correct: but Penn was then only 39, and his dress is that of a Quaker of West's boyhood. 99

He intended to call the new colony 'Sylvania', because of the forests; but the king insisted on '*Penn*sylvania', in memory of his old friend the admiral. When it was learned that Penn was determined to have no soldiers, no arms, no forts, people said that the Holy Experiment would soon be destroyed by the Red-skins. In spite of these attacks, he was full of hope: 'God has given me this country in the face of the world', he said. 'He will bless it and make of it the seed of a nation.' The future was to confirm the faith shown by William Penn on this occasion: the Holy Experiment was to last three-quarters of a century, from 1682 to 1756.

Penn sent his cousin, Colonel Markham, to take possession of the province and treat with the Indians for the purchase of land; he considered them as legal owners, although the Crown had 'given' it to him. The name of the future city was already chosen by him: it was to be called Philadelphia—the City of Brotherly Love. William Penn set out from Deal on 1 September 1682, on the ship *Welcome*, accompanied by over a hundred Friends.

The colony made rapid growth after the conclusion, in 1683, of the Grand Treaty of Shackamaxon, between the natives and

Original plan of Philadelphia.

Philadelphia: the first Friends' meeting-house.

William Penn. This famous treaty was celebrated some forty years later in a long eulogy by Voltaire, the first sentence of which is often quoted: 'It is the only treaty between those nations and the Christians that was never sworn to and has never been broken. . . . They loved these newcomers as much as they hated the other Christians who were conquering and destroying America. . . . William Penn could boast of having brought into the world the Golden Age that people talk so much about, and that has probably only existed in Pennsylvania.' (*Lettre sur les Quakers.*) Won over by Penn's attitude, the Indians preserved for the man they called Onas (i.e. pen) a feeling of reverence that was handed down from generation to generation.

Penn said it was not easy to organize a form of government that suited all countries. 'Men side with their passions against their reason; wherefore governments rather depend upon men than men upon governments. Let men be good, and the government cannot be bad. If it be ill, they will cure it. . . . Though good laws do well, good men do better; for good laws may want good men, and be abolished or evaded by ill men.' Elsewhere he says that it is essential for the people to be taught to think and act nobly; in another place, that liberty without obedience is confusion, and obedience without freedom is slavery. Typical of his attitude to war, even in self-defence, is his statement that one must not fight, but suffer; faith and the practice of religion replace fighting.

The first article of Penn's Frame of Government, i.e. of the Constitution, naturally enough insisted on liberty of conscience: this, extended to Catholics, was unique in the British possessions. Authority emanated from the Governor, a hereditary leader representing the executive power, assisted by a Provincial Council and an Assembly. The Council consisted of seventy-two members, a third of them retiring each year, and, divided into committees, it prepared and brought forward bills and maintained public order. These committees were really Ministries. The Assembly was appointed for one year; its functions were restricted to ratifying or vetoing the actions of the Council. Broadly speaking, one might sum up the system as liberty of thought, inviolability of person and property, and popular control over all the powers of the State. The Constitution, devised by Penn, was accepted without much alteration; twenty-nine new laws were added, following the same humanitarian ideas. One of them required that every child of twelve should learn a useful trade; prisons were to be places of moral reformation, by teaching prisoners and making them work. The death penalty, at that time inflicted for some two hundred offences in England, was reserved for wilful murder, and later for treason also. Imprisonment for debt was gone. A man unjustly condemned received back double the fine he had paid. The property of a convicted criminal was to be confiscated, and divided between his own family and the victim's. Bold innovations were thus quietly made. In three days, the Constitution and the laws were passed.

The capital, Philadelphia, was laid out according to the plans of William Penn, with broad, straight streets running at right angles to one another, bearing the names of trees (Walnut

Philadelphia: the market-place in the 18th century.

Street, Spruce Street, etc.) or numbers (Second Street, Fifth Street, etc.), for the sake of simplicity, except for two main avenues a hundred feet wide, named Broad Street and High (now Market) Street, which cross in the centre of Philadelphia, where now stands the great City Hall, with its cupola surmounted by the massive statue of the founder. In spite of his heavy tasks of administration, William Penn regularly went to meeting for worship twice a week and often spoke. Philadelphia soon had the name of the 'green city', because of the large amount of space left for trees and grass. Three years after Penn had landed, the town had 600 houses and two schools.

Such surprising success quickly aroused envy at home: the cordial relations between the settlers and the Indians were as astonishing as the quick growth in population and cultivation. Penn had to return to England on legal business in 1684. Charles II died soon after; his younger brother James II, an avowed Catholic, morose and bigoted, continued to honour his promise to the dying Admiral Penn that he would befriend William; but his friendship made life increasingly difficult for Penn. Meanwhile Penn used his influence over the king in favour of persecuted Friends and others. For long unaware of calumny directed against himself, Penn had to defend himself with determination, but was unable to wash away the stain

An Indian village on Roanoke Island in the 1580s, by John White.
1. *Chief's house;* 2. *Altar;* 3. *Ritual dance;* 4. *Feast;*
5. *Tobacco and sunflowers; Corn-guardian's hut;* 7. *Wheat-field;*
8. *Pumpkins;* 9. *Ritual fire;* 10. *Pond.*

of slander. He was sent to Holland, as English ambassador to William of Orange, but had to come back in a hurry when the Dutchman invaded England. James fled; and William became king. The new government arrested Penn; released on bail, he was later pardoned. Although he had sold lands to the Pennsylvania settlers at one-fifth of the market price, they would pay him no quit-rent; this nearly ruined him. William III wanted to take over the colony, to defend it against the French from Canada and the Mississippi. Penn was at last about to leave for America when a message from George Fox recalled him to London. He found Fox on his death-bed, and was with him at the last, on 13 January 1691.

Further accusations were made; Penn had to put off his departure once more; the Crown intervened and took from him the government of Pennsylvania. It was a hard blow. Some time later, William III restored it to him, and he was cleared of all the charges against him. His wife died, worn out by all this anxiety, and bitter was his grief. It was about this time that he wrote *Some Fruits of Solitude*, a little volume of thoughts and maxims, and later his *Essay towards the Present and Future Peace of Europe*, in which a convincing plan for a league of nations is

Centre section of one of the wampum belts, made of white and violet beads, given to Penn by the Indians, and used in negotiations with them. This one is now in the collection of the Historical Society of Pennsylvania.

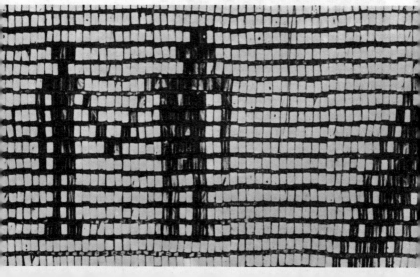

set forth at length. He suggested a congress of European nations, before which all members should bring their disputes, and whose decisions should be binding; thus peace would be guaranteed if only kings and statesmen would try it. In a law thesis which appeared in 1926, a Japanese student, Taro Terasaki, noted that Penn was more than just an Englishman: although he was English, and perhaps American too, as founder of Pennsylvania, belonging to that British race which dislikes logic and abstract thought, he was more than that. Penn once said to an English friend who was expressing admiration for his great learning, that he supposed it was due to his being educated at Saumur. Taro Terasaki adds: 'He is something of a Frenchman in his ideas, notably in unhesitatingly adopting the idea of sanctions in his plan for a League of Nations.' It is to be remembered that his essay on Peace came out twenty years before the work on the same subject by the Abbé de Saint-Pierre, whose *Projet de Paix Perpétuelle* is better known in France than Penn's essay.

His reappointment as Governor (9 August 1694) was a first ray of light; but his elder son died at the age of twenty, and

Philadelphia: the house given by Penn to his daughter Letitia.

neither his young wife (he had recently remarried) nor his children were willing to leave England. These personal troubles were invaded by alarming news of an impending crisis in Pennsylvania. To deal with the threat, Penn took ship on 9 September 1699. It was seventeen years since he had for the first time landed on that empty shore, where now new towns were springing up as if by magic. In spite of this marvellous transformation

Francis Place painted this portrait in 1696.
It is thought by some to be of William Penn.

he was filled with melancholy; the material prosperity of Philadelphia did not console him for the sorrows that are common to
man. If Penn had submitted his work to impartial examination
he would perhaps have recognized that he was largely to blame
for the troublesome situation of which he complained. The
difficulties caused by his long years of absence in England were
made worse by his being a curiously bad judge of character in
men: he seemed to take them at their own valuation and had
chosen the wrong men for office in Pennsylvania. Now that he
had come, his great influence was sufficient to quell conflict.
Apart from struggling with his parliament, he was preoccupied
by two questions: negro slavery and relations with the Red
Indians. To start with, he had accepted slavery as a temporary
evil that needed to be remedied gradually; but all he could do
now was to free all his black 'servants'; most of the colonists
considered the abolition of slavery a Utopian idea. As the
Crown now wanted to annex Pennsylvania, Penn had to set off
for England again, to take up the defence of their common
interests. As the Assembly had refused to pay his passage, he
had to sell land to find the money. It was the Redskins who gave
him his reward: they came in haste from all parts of the province to wish him good-bye. The farewell so moved the Indians
that a hundred years later the memory of this scene was still
vivid among their descendants.

William Penn had seen the land of the Holy Experiment for
the last time.

His government survived. He granted a revised constitution
in 1701, commemorated by the Liberty Bell. Until 1756, the
Quakers presided over the destinies of the colony, although after
1700 they no longer formed the majority of the nation. In 1756,
at the outbreak of the Seven Years War, the Governor declared
war on the Indians, and Friends withdrew from the Assembly.
Despite that, however, the Quaker Party remained very influential until the outbreak of the War of American Independence in 1776.

Innumerable troubles awaited Penn on his return to England.
His trusted agent had been cheating him, unsuspected, for

years; the agent's widow sued him for £16,000, and he had to go to prison for debt, until the whole sordid conspiracy was unravelled. He was old and weary. Early in 1712 a stroke put an end to his writing, and almost completely to speech and thought as well. A child's mind remained, and his gentle smile. He died on 30 July 1718, aged seventy-four.

Few people have been so exposed to criticism as William Penn, the Quaker courtier. The enemies of Quakerism and of the Restoration Court vigorously condemned his compromises and his apparent inconsistencies. Macaulay the historian echoed these slanders, but admitted that he would always be mentioned with honour as the founder of a colony which, in its relations with a savage people, did not abuse the power that is given by civilization. So far as we can examine the facts objectively, it is not for us to condemn Penn. His chief weaknesses were his lack of understanding of character in choosing his collaborators, and his exaggerated Quaker optimism not always counterbalanced by prudence and practical sense. Too often he preferred to temporize, even if inaction left uncertainty in the minds of those about him. On the other hand, intellectually, he was one of the most gifted men of his time. He was capable of great conceptions like the United States of America and the League of Nations. His was a most charming personality. 'I know no religion', he said, 'which destroys courtesy, civility and benevolence.'

> The career of William Penn, marred as it is with faults of timidity and imperfect judgement, is yet one that shows most instructively how the Quaker saint *can* bring his religion into public life and make it influence affairs of State for the wellbeing of a great community. He was a true statesman as well as a prophet of the Inward Light. He anticipated some of the principles of statesmanship that we are slowly learning, and others that the world has not learned yet. . . . His memory must be revered as the first statesman who had the faith and courage to make belief in the Inward Light in the souls of men the basic principle of the government of a great community.[1]

[1] Grubb, op. cit., p. 148.

George Fox—the Closing Years

In Fox's *Journal* we find the following passage, describing what happened on his return from Ireland in 1669:

> I had seen from the Lord a considerable time before that I should take Margaret Fell to be my wife. And when I first mentioned it to her, she felt the answer of life from God thereunto . . . people had long talked of it, and there was some jumble in some minds about it. . . . When her daughters were come, I asked both them and her sons-in-law if they had anything against it, or for it; and they all severally expressed their satisfaction therein. So after I had thus acquainted the children with it, our intention of marriage was laid before Friends, both privately and publicly, to their full satisfaction, many of whom gave testimony thereunto that it was of God. Afterwards, a meeting being appointed for the accomplishing thereof, in the public meeting-house at Broadmead in Bristol, we took each other, the Lord joining us together in the honourable marriage, in the everlasting covenant and immortal seed of life. Then was a certificate relating both to the proceedings and the marriage openly read. . . .[1]

It is recorded that the marriage certificate was signed by ninety-four Friends present. George Fox went on with his journeys about the country whilst his wife was arrested and imprisoned at Lancaster. Fortunately the king had her set at liberty just before Fox left for America. We have seen that he stayed there from 1671 to 1673, came back to England, and was imprisoned at Worcester: this caused his mother's death, for she had so much wanted to see her son again before she died. After more than a year's detention, he was acquitted, and went to settle at Swarthmoor in June 1675. He was fifty-one, and it was the first time in thirty-two years that he was living in his own home. He stayed there nearly two years, receiving visits from his friends—amongst them William Penn—setting his papers in order, taking part in meetings for church affairs and for worship in various places. It was the first rest he had allowed

[1] *Journal* (Everyman's Library edn., 1924), p. 263.

Swarthmoor Hall
The room where Friends held their meetings from
1652 to 1690. The panelling was restored in 1914.

A bedroom: the panelling and fireplace are original.

himself since the beginning of his mission. His health was no longer good, and he complained of weakness that was preventing him from travelling far in one day. In 1677, after three weeks spent at William Penn's house in Sussex, he set off for Holland and Germany, as we have already related. On his return, he lived in London for nearly a year, then came back to Swarthmoor, where he spent a year and a half: it was the last time he stayed there. In 1684 he went to Holland for seven weeks, and came back to settle down in the London district for the remainder of his life. He became steadily weaker, and his health was obviously declining. He often visited the schools. During the last year of his life, his wife, aged seventy-six, came to see him in London once again, and stayed with him nearly three months. Until the end, he was continually dictating letters on behalf of his cause and of other people.

A letter from William Penn to Margaret Fox, dated 13th 11th month 1690—i.e 13 January 1691, as the year then began on 25 March—written on the day her husband died, runs as follows:

Dear M. Fox,—With the dear remembrance of my unfeigned love in Xt Jesus, I am to be the teller to thee of sorrowful tidings as I may call it in some sense, which is this, that thy dear husband and my beloved and dear friend, G. Fox, has finished his glorious testimony this night about half an hour after nine, being sensible to the last breath.

Oh, he is gone, and has left us in the storm that is over our heads, surely in great mercy to him, but as an evidence to us of sorrows to come. He was as living and firm Fourth Day last was a week at Gracechurch Street, and this last First Day, being the day before yesterday, but complained after meeting of being inwardly struck,[1] and lay ever since at Henry Goldney's where he departed.

My soul is deeply affected with this hasty, great loss. Surely it portends to us great evils to come. A prince indeed is fallen in Israel to-day.

[1] At the end of that meeting, he made the following remark: 'I am glad I was here. Now I am clear, I am fully clear.'

I cannot enlarge for I shall write to several to-night and it is late. The Lord be with thee and thine, and us all. Amen.

I am thy faithful and affectionate Friend,

WM. PENN

His funeral was imposing and solemn in its simplicity. The Meeting for Worship lasted two hours, and two thousand persons were present. The burial took place in London, at the Friends' Burial Ground at Bunhill Fields, where a simple tablet now commemorates him.

Most of George Fox's writings, as well as some of the books that composed his own library, are preserved in the Library at Friends' House, London.

To conclude the first part of this study, it is appropriate to quote again from Rufus M. Jones's Introduction to the *Journal*, while bearing in mind that the criticism is based on what Fox showed himself to be in his *Journal*, his epistles, his many pamphlets, and his private correspondence.

Fox reveals in his own biographical accounts an unstable psychic constitution, very much like that which comes to light in the biographies of many other mystics and prophets. Scholars have coined technical terms to describe the phases of this condition, but neither these terms nor the scientific diagnosis of his case and kindred cases gives us much real light on the peculiar condition which seems to favour the formation of a certain type of spiritual leader and which appears to make the person in question uniquely sensitive to divine currents as well as a magnetic influence over other lives.

. . . I always wish that he had not taken so much satisfaction in the 'judgements' which overtook many of the persons that persecuted him. It would have been better if he could have shown more tenderness and gentle sweetness toward those who made his life thorny and dolorous, but this is to ask for a state of perfection to which few attain. It is, however, to be noted that in many cases he won the love and appreciation of his judges and his jailers, and in quite a number of instances they became 'convinced' of the truth of his message and joined his fellowship.

GEORGE FOX,
BORN
7TH Mo 1624,
DIED 13TH OF 11TH Mo 1690,
AGED 66 YEARS.

Near Bunhill Fields cemetery in London is the little Friends' burial-ground, surrounded now by factories and bombed sites. A new stone slab, replacing this headstone, records the fact that thousands of Friends were buried there. The Old Style calendar, with the year ending on March 24th, was in use in England until 1752. Fox died on January 13th, 1691.

In Gr......n Stool
Half dram half fool!

With a sigh, or a squeak, or a grunt, or a groan

'The Quakers wait for inspiration.'
An English caricature of the 19th century.

The Period of Quietism (1725-1825)

At the end of the seventeenth century, as we have already said (p. 81), there were at least 50,000 Quakers in England and Ireland. As persecution had ceased, an increase in numbers was to be expected. But that did not occur. Numbers declined; a hundred years after Fox's death, there were only 20,000 Quakers in England. Let us examine the causes of this decline.

Firstly, persecution and emigration had taken their toll. The original leaders had died. Their enthusiasm, and their vision of Quakerism as the world-religion, were replaced by a quiet, deep concern for personal holiness, and for maintaining the witness of the Society. Secondly, they were very successful in trade and industry, and lived frugally; thus many grew rich; and riches cooled their spiritual fire. The missionary spirit slackened; matters of discipline, dress, and speech took the place of the great affirmations of religion. They turned their eyes inward, seeking to keep themselves unspotted from the world. A kind of Quietism overcame the Society of Friends.

The Quaker religion of the first period represented a living union between the mystical and the evangelical aspects of Christianity, both in doctrine and in practice: in doctrine, because no theological opinion was valid unless it was related to a direct religious experience; in practice, as any outward activity was valueless unless under immediate inspiration. The peculiar power of the early Quakers was due at least in part to the balance they held between the internal and external forces of religious life.

The creative period was thus followed by a conservative period. Its hallmark was Quietism, that European movement of spiritual self-discipline that has exerted such power ever since the seventeenth century. Thomas à Kempis's book, *Of the Imitation of Christ*, was and still is one of the most influential works in this vein. This sentence from a letter by the Spanish mystic Falconi (1628) comes near to the core of Quietist thinking: 'Dwell in silence. Think of nothing, however good, however sublime it may be. Dwell only in pure faith in God and in utter resignation to His Holy will.'[1] Such concentration of mind and will were fostered by the reading of Barclay's *Apology*, to name only one of the books a Quaker household would read; and, inevitably, Quakers absorbed something of the spiritual climate of Quietism that was abroad in the land. From 1772, when the Quaker James Gough produced a translation of the writings of Madame Guyon, Friends became familiar with Continental exponents of these ideas: the Spanish-Italian monk Molinos and the French Bishop Fénelon should be mentioned with Madame Guyon.

This period of Quietism was remarkable, in the Society of Friends, for a great number of men and women of noble character and considerable achievement who have left an enduring monument in the life of mankind. Three well-known

[1] R. M. Jones, *Later Periods of Quakerism*, p. 41.

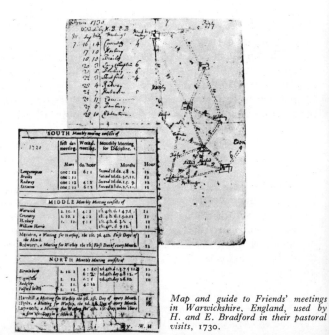

Map and guide to Friends' meetings in Warwickshire, England, used by H. and E. Bradford in their pastoral visits, 1730.

Philadelphia in the 18th century: the meeting-house on High Street (now Market Street).

names may be mentioned: John Woolman of America, Elizabeth Fry of England, and Anthony Benezet, who was born in France (see Chapter XIII). During this time, Quakers governed three American colonies and were active in the politics of two others. We have seen, in the chapter on the Quakers in America, that the Golden Age of the Society of Friends in that country came between 1700 and 1740, with Philadelphia at the height of its importance. On the other hand, the internal 'discipline' of the Society had taken shape over the years. Members were 'disowned for marrying out', i.e. were cast out of the Society for marrying a person not in membership; and this caused immense losses in numbers and in the quality of members. J. S. Rowntree pointed out in 1859 that, of the English Friends who had married in the preceding fifty years, five thousand, or one-third of the total, had been disowned for marrying out. It became an intolerably heavy price to pay for family unity in religious life.

It was also a period of mysticism: the spoken ministry in

(top) *Caricature of an English Quaker, by the French artist Daumier (1808–79).*

(lower) *Silhouette of the American Friend Dr. Joseph Parrish (1779–1840).*

Meeting insisted on obedience to the secret leadings of the Spirit of God. Many Friends had an unexpected, inward call to travel, visiting Quaker families and Meetings. They travelled thousands of miles, for months or years on end; some got to know virtually every Meeting in the American colonies; another became the personal friend of the Czar of Russia—the list could go on for pages. They went on unplanned journeys, as the Spirit told them, but always with the approval of their home Meeting, and if travelling among Friends, with the approval of the Meetings they were visiting. Generally they paid their own expenses and at the same time provided for their families; if necessary, their home Meeting would help. These itinerant Friends, most prominent in the Society between 1775 and 1825, linked the Society together and gave it some sort of uniformity.

At the same time, the Friends appointed to be responsible for discipline in the Society grew too important: the priest out-weighed the prophet. It is therefore not surprising that, in that

There were many caricatures of William Allen (see pp. 128, 133): this is a comparatively mild one of him chasing his third wife-to-be to their wedding at Stoke Newington.

same half-century, Friends came to question their methods and their Quietism. Although in England the Society managed to retain different points of view within its borders, the American Quaker movement split up, at first in the Philadelphia district (1827–9). The separation was caused partly by questions of discipline, and partly by a fundamental disagreement on theology: is man born with the Seed of God within him, with an Inner Light—the traditional Quaker view—or is he by nature wholly sinful, only to be saved by the grace of God?—the Evangelical view. The American separation in Philadelphia lasted until 1955.

The spiritual drowsiness of the eighteenth century was not peculiar to Friends; it applied to English religious life as a whole. It was John Wesley (1703–91) and his associates in the Methodist Revival who shook up the churches and set them on the move again.

Many American Quaker homes were stations on the Underground Railroad helping negroes to escape to freedom in the northern states.

Until the middle of the nineteenth century, the Quakers were a caste apart, a peculiar people. They hardly mingled with 'the world' at all. In England the universities were closed to them, as to all Non-conformists. The first Quaker was admitted to the House of Commons in 1833. By their way of life, their dress, their manners, their theeing-and-thouing (the 'plain speech'), they formed a society within Society. Yet originally Quakers had only been seeking modesty and simplicity; from the end of the seventeenth century, in their efforts to fight the tyranny of Dame Fashion, they had made their simple clothes into a fixed uniform. A characteristic Quaker dress virtually disappeared in England at the beginning of this century, but can still be seen among Friends in some parts of America.

Although the Society of Friends in England seemed to be half-asleep in its religious thinking during this period, much fine educational work was done. A Quaker school was founded at Ackworth in Yorkshire in 1779. The success of this boarding-school for boys and girls led to the establishment of similar schools, notably at Westtown, Pennsylvania, in 1799, and gradually Friends gained a reputation for the way they educated their children. With the lead given by that improvident genius Joseph Lancaster, they led the way towards universal primary education in England. In 1807, they helped Wilberforce in his struggle against slavery. Joseph Pease was the first Quaker to sit in the House of Commons; his son Edward was the 'Father of Railways'. Led by Elizabeth Fry, Friends took an active part in prison reform; and the first hospital for the rational treatment of the insane was founded at York in 1792 by a Quaker, William Tuke.

Some Prominent Quakers of the Eighteenth and Nineteenth Centuries

Although the reading public in France took a lively interest in Quakerism all through the eighteenth century, few Frenchmen joined the movement. Their admiration came chiefly to be directed to Pennsylvania as a heaven-upon-earth. Two Friends who made their mark in the Society were however French by birth: Anthony Benezet and Stephen Grellet.

Antoine Bénézet was born at Saint-Quentin (where there is a street named after him) on 31 January 1713. His family were Protestants, originally southerners, from the Languedoc. When he was two, they fled to Holland, then to England. When he was about fourteen, Anthony began to go to Friends' meetings, and became a member. In 1731 the Benezet family landed in America, and Anthony married in 1736. Living at Philadelphia, he soon devoted himself to teaching children, and took charge of a section of the William Penn Charter School. In 1755 he founded a girls' school of his own. He was ahead of his time in methods of education, and introduced new ideas in the teaching of the deaf and dumb. The sad lot of the negro slaves engaged his attention; about 1750 he opened at his own expense an evening school for negroes, and taught them to read and write. Benezet then took up work for the abolition of the slave-trade, and became an unpaid journalist. From 1762 to 1767 he published at his own expense three books on this subject. He got into touch with Benjamin Franklin, John Wesley, and other important people who could influence public opinion on both sides of the Atlantic. In 1775 he was largely responsible for founding the Pennsylvania Society for Promoting the Abolition of Slavery, for the Relief of Free Negroes Unlawfully Held in Bondage, and for Improving the Conditions of the African Race. Writing to the Abbé Raynal in 1781, he added, 'How desirable it would be if Louis XVI gave the example to other potentates, by forbidding his subjects to engage in the slave trade.' In 1783 he wrote to

Queen Marie Antoinette and to the queens of England and Portugal. He had the joy of living to see all members of the Society of Friends in Pennsylvania emancipate the slaves they held. He was a personal friend of John Woolman.

All this activity was not enough for him. As war filled his Christian heart with grief, he wrote books and pamphlets entreating men to give up killing one another. He also took an interest in the lot of the Red Indians, founding an association for their benefit in 1756. He took up the cause of the Acadians

This silhouette was lithographed often with the words 'Thy nearly attached Friend Stephen Grellet'; ——in modern English: 'Your devoted Friend'.

(see Longfellow's poem *Evangeline*, 1847); their province, Acadia (now Nova Scotia), had been ceded by France to England in 1713, and the commander of the British forces had decided on their mass deportation; they numbered 7,000. As two or three hundred of these unfortunate people tried to escape, the country was laid waste and the fugitives almost all exterminated. Benezet set forth the situation to the king of England; five hundred Acadians were brought to Philadelphia, where he 'adopted' them and gave them all possible help. Apart from all these occupations and activities, he took a great interest in promoting the use of a French device for resuscitating the apparently drowned, using artificial respiration. He also published several books and pamphlets in English and French, publicizing the principles of the Society of Friends. He died on 3 May 1784. An immense number of people attended his funeral; hundreds of negroes were there. His friends had wanted a memorial written of him; but all he suggested was, 'Anthony Benezet was a poor creature, and, through Divine favor, was enabled to know it.'

Étienne de Grellet du Mabillier, later known as Stephen Grellet, was born at Limoges on 2 November 1773, the son of a

126   *There is unfortunately no authentic portrait of John Woolman. This may even be a portrait of Anthony Benezet who was 'notoriously ugly'. Janet Whitney discusses this picture in her* John Woolman, *p. 420.*

rich noble who owned porcelain factories and who was for some years comptroller of the Mint and an intimate friend of Louis XVI. He received a good education. On the outbreak of the French Revolution, the family property was confiscated, and the parents were put in prison. Stephen Grellet joined the Royalist army of *émigrés*, and was taken prisoner. He managed to escape to Demerara, and from there he made his way to New York. He had thrown off his Roman Catholic faith, and became an ardent admirer of Voltaire; consequently he admired William Penn. Although ignorant of English, he read some of Penn's writings with the help of a dictionary, started going to Friends' meetings, and went through a most intense conversion to Quakerism. He became a 'recorded minister', and felt a clear call to go to Philadelphia where yellow fever was raging, and where, know-

ing he was going to catch the disease himself, he ministered to the sick and dying. In the following ten years he frequently left home to travel in the ministry, and on four occasions he came to Europe, each time visiting the little groups of French Quakers near Nimes in the south of France. In 1807 he visited French monasteries and convents; in 1811 he was in England, visiting prisons: after seeing women and babies in Newgate

I went to Mildred's Court, to my much valued friend, Elizabeth J. Fry, to whom I described, out of the fulness of my heart, what I had just beheld, stating also that something must be done immediately for those poor suffering children. The appeal to

John G. Whittier, the great American poet and abolitionist.

Jerry Barrett's picture of Elizabeth Fry visiting the prisoners at Newgate.

such a pious and sensible [sensitive] mind as dear Elizabeth possesses, was not in vain. She immediately sent for several pieces of flannel, and had speedily collected a number of our young women Friends, who went to work with such diligence, that on the very next day she repaired to the prison with a bundle of made-up garments for the naked children. What she then saw of the wretchedness of that prison induced her to devise some plan towards the amelioration of the condition of those poor women, and, if possible, the reform of their morals, and instilling into their minds the principles and love of the Christian religion. . . .

In 1813–14 Stephen Grellet travelled in France, Switzerland, and Germany, amid the horrors and confusion of war. In 1818, with William Allen, he set out for Scandinavia and Russia, where they renewed their acquaintance (begun in London) with Czar Alexander, and advised him on prison reform. Returning via Greece, Stephen Grellet went to Rome, where he inspected the secret records of the Inquisition and had a very cordial interview with the Pope. In 1831–4 he travelled as far as Hungary and Spain. He died on 16 November 1855, at the age of eighty-two. He was known as the 'ambassador of Christ'; he found it easy to meet and converse with kings, and he only travelled when and where he felt the clear urging of his Master.

John Woolman is another man who should be called a saint. It can truly be said that he had unshakeable faith, unparalleled simplicity and humility, a desire for absolute truth, and immense love for the whole creation. He is chiefly known for his unremitting fight against negro slavery. He was born on 19 October 1720 in West New Jersey, not far from Philadelphia.

The travelling Quaker ministers of this period all left Journals for the edification of those who came after them; these Journals could be found in every Quaker household. It is John Woolman's *Journal* that became the classic of its kind, partly because of its rare beauty of style. He had a happy boyhood, was sensitive to the things of God, and was full of fun as an adolescent. At the age of twenty, he began to speak in Quaker meetings. He left his father's farm, and became the assistant in a shop that also handled minor legal business. Here is the well-known passage (at the end of Chapter I) in which he tells how he was awakened to his life-work:

Within a year after my coming to Mount Holly my master having a negro sold her and told me to write a bill of sale. The thoughts of writing an instrument of slavery for one of my fellow creatures gave me trouble, and I was distressed in my mind about it. At length I considered that I was hired by the year, it was my master bid me do it, and that it was an elderly man, a member of our Society, who bought her, so I wrote the bill of sale. But at the executing of it I was depressed in my mind, and said before my master and the Friend that I believed slave-keeping to be a practice inconsistent with the Christian religion; saying so abated my uneasiness; yet as often as I reflected seriously upon it, I thought I should have been clearer if leaving all consequences, I had craved to be excused from it, as a thing against my conscience; for such it was.

He became a tailor, and earned his keep by that trade for the rest of his life. On his many journeys as a Quaker minister he visited the important Quaker planters, urging them to give up slavery. With firmness and tact he tried to convince his hearers of their error and awaken sympathy for the slaves. In the 1758 Yearly Meeting at Philadelphia he won over most of the Friends who still favoured slave-holding. He went on tirelessly with his journeys on foot or on horseback, amidst all the dangers of travel on that continent. In 1776, after his death, and thanks to his efforts and those of Friends whom he and Anthony Benezet had inspired, the Society of Friends in Philadelphia said that they would disown any Friends who had not freed all their negroes.

L'Assemblee des Coüacres

A French caricature of a Quaker meeting, adapted from Hemskerck's painting. Underneath is given a reasonably fair summary of Quaker peculiarities.

The liberation was completed by about 1784; the first Quaker protests against slavery having been made in 1675 and 1688.

Wishing to visit Friends in England, John Woolman embarked on 1 May 1772. In England he was struck by the wretched circumstances of the labouring classes. He caught smallpox and died at York on 7 October of that year, far from his country, his wife and his children. Apart from his *Journal*, he left a number of writings including *A Plea for the Poor: or, A Word of remembrance and caution to the Rich* (1793).

Elizabeth Fry, whose name is known all over the world, was born on 21 May 1780, into the Gurney family of Norwich. She married in 1800 and had eleven children. A lover of bright clothes and amusements in her youth, she had become deeply religious by the time of her marriage, but never lost her tolerance. For the rest of her life she was an enlightened Quaker minister, whose addresses and prayers were the comfort of all. Elizabeth Fry's outstanding achievement was the reform of prisons, which had remained in an appalling state. As has been already mentioned, Stephen Grellet had drawn her attention to the problem after visiting Newgate prison in London. She had brought clothes—and hope—to the women of Newgate in 1811. She did not go there again until January 1817, when she went alone into the howling mob of women, gently picked up a child, and was listened to in tearful silence as she suggested that one of the prisoners should teach the children to read and write. The behaviour of the prisoners was transformed at once. The

In several villages near Nimes, in the south of France, isolated groups of Protestants joined London Yearly Meeting before the French Revolution.

PRÉCIS

DES

RÈGLES DE DISCIPLINE CHRÉTIENNE,

ADOPTÉES

PAR LA SOCIÉTÉ DES AMIS,

CONNUS SOUS LE NOM

DE QUAKERS,

DE CONGENIÉS,

ET AUTRES LIEUX ENVIRONNANS,

Dans les années 1785, 1801 et 1807.

school flourished. Elizabeth Fry became the guardian angel of the women prisoners whom she and her friends taught to sew, read, and write. She would read the Bible to them, talk and pray with them. She protested against the Howard system of solitary confinement which she considered inhuman and a grave mistake; she insisted on women prisoners having women warders, on prisoners being classified according to their crimes, and on their being together by day but not herded together at night. Her heart and her intelligence, and not any specialized study, had taught her the new methods which she fostered with all her strength.

Janet Whitney, in her biography,[1] says: 'So casually and simply Elizabeth Fry began a work which within a few months had grown to a dimension which carried her name all over the country, within three years was to place her in correspondence, as prison adviser, with most of the crowned heads of Europe, and

[1] *Elizabeth Fry, Quaker Heroine* (1937).

Meeting-house and burial-ground of the Friends at Congenies near Nimes. The group died out in the 19th century, owing to conscription and emigration.

which since her death has given her a niche among the great women of history.' She set prison reform in motion in all civilized countries, took an effective interest in the women convicts turned loose from the transports at Botany Bay in Australia, persuaded the authorities to prohibit *suttee* (the custom of widows committing suicide) in British India, set up a training-school for nurses in London, organized libraries for the 500 coastguard stations in Britain, and all the time cared for her husband and her eleven children. She died at Ramsgate in 1845 at the age of sixty-five.

The many Quakers who made a distinguished contribution to science or education in the eighteenth and nineteenth centuries include Thomas Young (1773–1829), doctor and scientist; John Dalton (1766–1844), physician, chemist, and ophthalmologist; Dr. John Fothergill (1712–80); Dr. Thomas Hodgkin, pathologist (Hodgkin's disease); J. Hutchinson (1811–61), a well-known dermatologist; Lord Lister (1827–1912), the famous surgeon whose work on antiseptics revolutionized surgery; Lindley Murray (1745–1826), who has been called the 'father of English grammar'; Joseph Lancaster (1771–1838), whose work for popular education has already been mentioned; Joseph Sturge, of Birmingham, who started the first Adult Schools in 1845, and saw their membership reach 50,000 before he died fifty years later; and William Allen (1770–1843), who was a chemist, physician, geologist, and astronomer, and accompanied Stephen Grellet to Russia.

Quaker relief: a transport team at Caen in France at the end of the Second World War.

Quakerism in the Modern World

In the next few pages we shall attempt to assess the development of the Quaker movement in the past hundred years, what causes it has sponsored in this present century, what currents of thought are moving through it, and what promise the future holds.

In religious books published sixty to eighty years ago, it was common to see some such comment as the following: Quakers were first in the field in many movements, but there is little point in their continued existence nowadays; the reforms they were so enthusiastic about have been generally achieved: the abolition of slavery, the emancipation of women, penal reform, the peace movement, and so on, have become a part of civilized life and nobody argues about them now; the Quakers have fulfilled their task; they may as well disappear!

Unfortunately progress has not been so smooth; in many

Hospital Train sent to Russia by the Friends Service Committee at the end of th First World War.

respects the world has gone backwards to barbarism. Two world wars and their dreadful aftermath—the double threat of the bomb and of starvation—have shown the need for groups of men and women who are convinced that spiritual things must come first, and that human life and conscience are sacred.

The Society of Friends has opened its doors to the influences of modern thought and discoveries. The old concepts of individual philanthropy have, in the thinking of younger generations, made way for more broadly social ideas. In the United States more than 150 new Quaker groups have come into being since 1925; and on the continent of Europe the various independent Yearly Meetings that have sprung up are of similarly recent growth. Let us consider further this social and international activity that has brought fresh life into the Quaker movement in the world.

English in origin, the Society of Friends has spread to many parts of the world; since 1937 there has been a Friends' World Committee for Consultation, having no executive authority but co-ordinating national Yearly Meetings. From 1954 to 1956 the Secretary of the World Committee was an Indian. The number of Friends in the world is over 174,000, of whom nearly

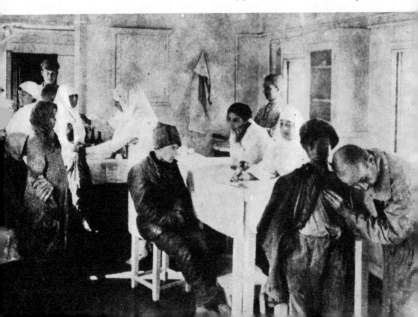

58,000 are outside the U.S.A. Three World Conferences have been held in the past thirty-five years, the first in London in 1920, the second near Philadelphia in 1937, and the third in England again at Oxford in 1952. About a thousand representatives took part in these meetings. Small European conferences have taken place almost every year since 1931, except during the war, for studying present-day problems in the light of the Gospel. A European Conference on a larger scale was held in England at Birmingham, in 1957, when over two hundred representatives from fourteen countries met to discuss the theme 'Through Fellowship to Action'. Half the representatives came from abroad: despite differences of background and difficulties of language, a warm fellowship was at once obvious.

All these changes have proceeded from 'Quaker international service', a practical, modern expression of the words of George Fox in Launceston gaol:

> Let all nations hear the word by sound or writing. Spare no place, spare not tongue nor pen; but be obedient to the Lord God and go through the work and be valiant for the Truth upon earth; tread and trample all that is contrary under . . . be patterns, be examples in all countries, places, islands, nations, wherever you come; that your carriage and life may preach

among all sorts of people, and to them. Then you will come to walk cheerfully over the world, answering that of God in every one (p. 263).

The year 1868 saw the first English Quaker organization formed for foreign missions. British Friends went to Madagascar. They went to China in 1886, and helped to found West China Union University in 1910, to Ceylon, the island of Pemba (near Zanzibar), Lebanon, India; American Friends shared some of this work, and went also to Alaska, Central America, Mexico, Japan, and Kenya. The spirit of Quaker missions was thus defined in the 1911 edition of *Christian Practice*: '. . . the sending of itinerant evangelists all over the world is not of itself sufficient. Beyond this, there is the need for patient work through all channels that can be used for exhibiting the spirit of Christ among the nations.' As this thought has been more and more borne in upon the Society, regular missionary work including medical, educational, and industrial departments, has been established. After the first World War, many young Friends felt uncomfortable at the thought of going to 'christianize' people belonging to civilizations as old as the Hindu or Chinese, whilst in Europe Christianity seemed to have lost its influence; for by their nationalism the Churches had proved that they had sunk to the position of being purely national churches, and that they had lost the universal message of Christ; once again their God had been transformed into a tribal god. One might add that the same thing happened during the second World War.

Turning to relief work, we remember that the Christian should be 'The repairer of the breach, The restorer of the paths to dwell in' (Is. 58: 12). At the end of the eighteenth century, after a rising in Ireland, English Friends organized relief for the refugees of both sides. During the Napoleonic Wars, help was given to the French prisoners in England, and also to the population in the devastated countryside of the German states. In 1856 relief work was done in Finland, where the British fleet had carried out a severe bombardment at the beginning of the Crimean War. We must not omit to mention the help given to

137

the French and German civilian populations during and after the Franco-Prussian War of 1870–1; clothing, seeds, furniture, steam tractors, etc., were sent to various parts of the east of France, the centre, the Loire, to Alsace and Lorraine, to Trier and Düsseldorf, and elsewhere. An appeal for funds raised about four million gold francs. The members of the Relief Committee were able to travel freely in both countries, thanks to passports issued by the French and German authorities. Relief was also sent to Russia during the terrible famines of 1891 and 1907.

From 1914 to 1919 an English relief committee gave help to German and Austrian civilians interned in England. More than 30,000 'enemy aliens' were thus aided on British soil. Relief was organized in six other countries; 1,800 English and American volunteers gave of their best, distributing food and equipment to the value of twenty-two million gold francs (sectional buildings, clothing, food, tools, maternity hospital at Châlons-sur-Marne, two temporary hospitals, etc., particularly for the parts of France that had been laid waste). In 1919 British and American Friends were the first to enter Germany as soon as the blockade was lifted. The work of relief and reconciliation reached its peak in 1923–4. In German cities a total of a million meals a day were served to children and students. A card was handed to the children who received this *Quäkerspeisung*, saying that 'Love and mutual aid, not violence and war, will bring peace and happiness to mankind.'

Quaker Relief (*Secours Quaker*) in France gave all the help it could to German Jewish refugees in France from 1933 onwards, and after the Germans had occupied the country in 1940 it took an interest in the French political prisoners held by the Germans; after the Liberation, in 1944, it worked for the French political prisoners detained for collaborating with the Germans. Material aid was given to war victims in the Paris region as well as in other cities. From 1940 to 1945 German Quakers, out of their slender resources, gave help to French prisoner-of-war camps near Berlin.

Although physical relief is important, Friends in all countries have long felt that such work is only a part of their task, and that their first duty is to give the war-torn world a spiritual message. As they feel their kinship with all men, they recognize their share of responsibility for the present state of the world. In order to be able to give this spiritual message in a permanent way, Friends have, since 1920, been setting up Quaker International Centres in various capitals on the continent of Europe and elsewhere; and they are largely responsible for the growth of new groups of Friends there. These centres have endeavoured to be places where people could learn to live in human fellowship, and to bring life to the spirits of men by new ideas, lectures, relief work, social service; by preaching the living Christ; and, as Children of Light, by proclaiming Love, which is the true substance of the Eternal. These ideas were first put forth by Carl Heath, who exerted a great influence upon Quakerism, both on the renewing of its thought and on the orientation of the whole movement. He had an unusual knowledge of European culture and thought, and was particularly fond of France, which he visited annually. He was also one of the architects of reconciliation between Britain and India. He was an expert on international questions, and was profoundly convinced of that aspect of Truth which Quakerism represents; he had become a member of the Society of Friends when he was grown up. Quakers of the twentieth century will remember him as the father of the new European Quakerism.

Friends' work for peace and international reconciliation has been recognized by the Committee of the Nobel Prize, which awarded the Peace Prize in 1946 to an American Friend, Emily G. Balch, and in 1947 to the two English and American Com-

Friends House, Euston Road, London.

mittees, the Friends' Service Council and the American Friends' Service Committee. One is reminded of Dr. Nansen's words, when he was speaking about Quaker relief in Russia during the great famines of 1921–2: 'By their forethought and their efforts, the Friends have prepared the way, as no other organization could do, for an international effort to save millions of Russians from famine . . . your devoted workers have re-kindled the spark of human love by their methods of personal contact, and once again the people are beginning to believe in human brotherhood which seemed extinct.'

FRANCE

In the early days of the movement, and during the first part of the eighteenth century, Quakers or *Couacres* were known to the reading public in France as oddities who allowed women to preach, who kept their hats on when meeting people, and spoke to everyone in the second person singular. Later, William Penn and Pennsylvania received fulsome admiration from philosophers who were propagating theories of equality and justice. This must have had some influence on the French Revolution at the end of the century, but it did not bring a single Quaker meeting into existence. An English Friend, part-owner of ships that had brought in French prizes in the American War of Inde-

pendence, advertised in Paris for the persons from whom those ships had been taken. This caused a stir, and brought English Friends into touch with groups of French Protestants near Nîmes, who had been following a line of thought and worship very similar to that of Friends ever since the beginning of the century. These groups united with London Yearly Meeting, but eventually died out, as conscription caused the younger men to emigrate. The Quaker International Centre was started in Paris in 1920, and books, pamphlets, and a monthly news-letter have been published. The first General Meeting was held in 1925, and they have been held annually ever since, even during the War. In 1932 and 1938 there were small conferences of French and German Friends at Bad Pyrmont in Germany, and just before the war broke out there was a conference of French, British, and American Friends at Honfleur (Calvados). France Yearly Meeting became independent in 1933.

Although there are fewer than a hundred French Friends, they have done significant work for Franco-German reconciliation, for penal reform and for juvenile delinquents;[1] they run an international circle for students in Paris and two small communities near Blois. Their friendliness and mutual tolerance are very striking.

GERMANY

A sketch of the history of Quakerism in Germany must begin with the deep springs of thought in the works of Meister Eckhardt, Tauler, Angelus Silesius, and of Jacob Böhme (1575–1624), and his English followers; they were all mystics and independent spiritual reformers. George Fox may not have read any of Böhme's writings, but their phraseology was common property in England and appears in his *Journal*. He and other Friends visited Germany and the Netherlands, and made the acquaintance of Mennonites, who are Christian pacifists with whom Quakers have much in common. Quaker groups grew up where there were Mennonites, e.g. in the Palatinate, the

[1] *Translator's note.* This work was largely inspired by Henry van Etten himself, who recently emigrated to America.

Arch Street meeting-house, Philadelphia, where the meeting for worship is based on silence. This photograph dates from before 1914.

Rhineland, at Hamburg, Emden, Danzig, and so on. These groups gradually disappeared about 1800; others then grew up at Minden and Bad Pyrmont, only to die out again towards the end of the nineteenth century; ever since the seventeenth century there had been a current of emigration to England and particularly to America, in search of religious and political freedom. Friends' relief work after the first World War revived interest in Quakerism; eighteen groups were in existence by 1928, and the International Centre was opened in Berlin. A monthly periodical and a large number of books are issued in German by Leonhard Friedrich's firm. The second World War found some German Friends already in concentration camps; and most men Friends were called up for service, but with non-combatant units; this may have been a coincidence. German Friends had had conferences in their meeting-house at Bad Pyrmont with French Quakers, to whom they were deeply attached; and since the war that meeting-house has been returned to them and is much used. There are now groups in both parts of Germany, with Friends endeavouring to bear their witness faithfully. The 1957 Yearly Meeting was held in the Eastern Zone, at Eisenach.

A meeting at Arch Street, 1955.

London Yearly Meeting has over 21,000 members, and 5,000 to 6,000 regular attenders not in membership, in more than 400 meetings. The headquarters of the Society has for the past thirty years been at Friends' House, opposite Euston Station in London, where there is the Library with its famous manuscripts, and the large meeting-house where the Yearly Meeting normally gathers to hear the Swarthmore Lecture, and during the ensuing week discuss the reports of the central committees that concentrate the concerns and activities of Friends. Such interests include education, international service, religious education in the broadest sense, social welfare, East–West relations, interracial relations, temperance, marriage and parenthood, penal reform, and peace. The chief of the Quaker periodicals is the weekly paper *The Friend*, now in its 116th year. Friends run nine boarding-schools (mostly co-educational) of which Yearly Meeting takes cognizance, and numerous other independent schools; over 1,000 Friends are teachers. An independent college for Quaker studies was founded in 1903 at Woodbrooke, Birmingham; and round it has grown up the group of Selly Oak Colleges, where Christians of various

denominations share the work of training men and women, notably for the mission field. Woodbrooke's chief aim is to give Friends the religious, social, and international education necessary for modern life; many foreign students and non-Friends come there to study. (In the United States, a similar institution was founded near Philadelphia in 1930 at Pendle Hill.)

Working against war and on behalf of better international relations is one of the chief activities of British Friends; and they have been actively engaged, both through their own movement and through such organizations as the Fellowship of Reconciliation and the Peace Pledge Union, in peace work and in defending the interests of conscientious objectors. During the 1914–18 War there were 16,000 objectors in Great Britain; in the second World War there were 60,000.[1] In 1916 a law was passed legalizing conscientious objection; but it did not prevent 270 Quakers from spending several years in prison, in conditions that were often very bad. In the second World War nearly 1,300 men Friends appeared before the Tribunals for conscientious objectors; upwards of 200 were exempted unconditionally and over 1,000 on various conditions, such as serving with the Friends' Ambulance Unit, which had done magnificent work in the first World War already (and which is due to close down when conscription ends). Many served prison sentences: meetings for worship were held in thirteen prisons. The small group of Quaker M.P.s have often put forward their Christian convictions when speaking in the House. On 25 November 1941, Dr. Arthur Salter, a Labour member, said, 'For centuries the Churches have sought to harmonize the Christian command "love one another" with the nationalist command "kill one another". If you fully accept Christ and his gospel, the two positions are wholly incompatible.'[2] Hatred, he said, was being engendered between nations by the Press and the B.B.C.

East–West tension is one of the great concerns of Friends; and

[1] The figures in this paragraph are from Elfrida Vipont, *The Story of Quakerism* (1954), p. 278.

[2] Fenner Brockway, *The Bermondsey Story* (1949), p. 231.

in 1951 they sent the first religious delegation to Soviet Russia. The very satisfactory reception it was given encouraged the sending of a similar delegation of Friends from the U.S.A. in 1955.

In conclusion we should mention that Oxford was the scene of the third World Conference of Friends, in August 1952. There were 900 representatives present, from all over the world. The general theme of the conference was the vocation of Friends in the modern world; and 1952 was the 300th anniversary of the birth of the Quaker movement, which proceeded from George Fox's vision on Pendle Hill in Lancashire. 'At Oxford', says Elfrida Vipont,[1] 'Friends were most deeply aware of their unity in diversity; of their international brotherhood, which might be a source of strength to Quaker service throughout the world; of their common discipleship in prayer and seeking; of the overwhelming importance of living in the spirit which takes away the occasion of all wars, and of the need for that spirit in a world still struggling in the ocean of darkness and death.'

UNITED STATES OF AMERICA

As has already been mentioned (p. 122), the American Quaker movement did not succeed in preserving its unity. Everywhere else in the world (with a few exceptions such as Kenya and Madagascar), Quakerism has continued to practise worship based on silence, with ministry devolving upon the meeting as a whole. This form is practised by scarcely more than one-third of the members in the U.S.A., being chiefly found in the Eastern States. In the Middle West and along the Pacific seaboard, a large part of the Society of Friends is known as the Friends' Church, not unlike the Methodist Church or other Protestant groups, except that it has maintained several of the great testimonies of Quakerism: that Jesus taught a *spiritual* religion, that outward sacraments are pointless, that it is wrong to take part in war, and so on. This Church supports full-time pastors; and its meetings for worship are ordinary Protestant services. On the other hand, this Friends' Church has, during

[1] *The Story of Quakerism*, p. 296.

the last forty years, given many leading personalities to non-pastoral Quakerism, as well as to the American Friends Service Committee. This Committee, since its foundation in 1917, has brought together Friends from most of American Quakerism into humanitarian work and into efforts to promote world peace. This common task has made it easier for a gradual converging of thought to occur. The two main branches of Philadelphia Friends united again in 1955. The following ground has recently been covered by the A.F.S.C.:

In the U.S.A.

Industrial, social, and political problems involving personal freedom; starting new industries to give work to unemployed miners; the American Indian programme in Arizona and South Dakota; prison visiting; the rights of conscience programme; services to conscientious objectors; peace education; radio service; work in schools and colleges; service units in mental hospitals and schools for the retarded and delinquent; work camps; work at the United Nations in New York.

In other Countries

International Centres at Paris, Geneva, Vienna, Dacca, Delhi, Amsterdam, Copenhagen, Tokio, Mexico City; conferences for diplomats in Switzerland and Ceylon; international student seminars in Austria, Denmark, England, Japan, Switzerland, and Yugoslavia; social and technical assistance in India, Jordan, and Italy; relief and rehabilitation in Korea; material aids to Austria, France, Germany, India, Italy, Japan, Jordan, Kenya, and Korea; aid to refugees in Europe and Korea; overseas work camps in Germany, Austria, Israel, Italy, Japan, and Kenya; school affiliation between various countries; and community service units in Mexico and El Salvador. This list is of course far from complete; and much of the work, such as aid to refugees, was also done at home, or in co-operation with Friends in other countries.

In conclusion it should be mentioned that American Friends run about forty schools and ten independent colleges and publish twenty-five periodicals, of which the two most important are the *Friends Journal* (Philadelphia, Pennsylvania) and *The American Friend* (Richmond, Indiana).

OTHER COUNTRIES

Ireland Yearly Meeting, founded in 1671, has about 2,000 members and two boarding-schools.

In Scandinavia, there are three small Yearly Meetings—in Denmark since 1879, with an International Centre in Copenhagen since 1939; in Stockholm since 1935: it is in touch with sympathizers in Finland; and in Norway, where the Meeting became independent of London Yearly Meeting about forty years ago. For the past twenty years, Scandinavian Friends have been linked together by one or two periodicals.

Switzerland has had an independent Yearly Meeting since 1947, with small groups in a number of towns and an International Centre that has played a significant part in the work of the League of Nations and the United Nations at Geneva. The movement in Switzerland owes very much to two Friends, Hélène Monastier, a teacher of Lausanne, who edits the monthly news-letter that draws Swiss Friends together, and the great pacifist Pierre Ceresole, who created the International Voluntary Service (Service Civil International) and who died in 1945.

In the Netherlands, there has been a Yearly Meeting since 1931; an International Centre was founded at Amsterdam in 1939; Friends are linked by a monthly news-letter.

In Austria, there has been an International Centre at Vienna since the end of the first World War, but the movement has never taken root.

In Russia, the Moscow Quaker Centre was gradually forced to close down about thirty years ago.

In China, Friends' work began effectively in 1886; by 1910 Chinese Friends had started several schools with Western assistance; and Friends were playing a responsible part in founding the West China Union University at Chengtu. American Friends built up pastoral meetings in Nanking, whilst

British Friends were responsible for an International Institute at Chungking, and for a Centre in Shanghai. The Friends' Ambulance Unit did substantial work in China during and after the second World War. The Friends' Mission to China in 1955, in their report published in London in 1957, gave a survey of the present position.

So far as India is concerned, in Delhi and in Dacca there are International Centres, in Calcutta a Quaker Office and in Madhya Pradesh and Orissa there is rural work. Regular meetings for worship are held at all these centres. There are other meetings in mid-India.

In Japan, the Yearly Meeting founded in 1917 with the help of American Friends had to dissolve itself in 1941, but came into existence again in 1948. There has been a very good girls' school in Tokyo since 1887. The small group of Japanese Quakers is very alive and active. Among Japanese Friends well known internationally are the late Inazo Nitobe, long connected with the League of Nations; Iwao Ayusawa, a former official of the International Labour Organization; and Tamon Maeda, well known in UNESCO.

There are small meetings in Jordan and the Lebanon, where the Friends' Schools at Ramallah and Brummana have always been able to preserve a degree of friendliness unusual in those countries among their pupils, who include Moslems and Druses as well as Christians—chiefly Maronites and Greek Orthodox. Friends also founded a hospital for mental diseases in the Lebanon.

There are Quaker meetings in Australia and New Zealand, with Friends' boarding-schools at Hobart in Tasmania and at Wanganui in New Zealand.

In the New World, apart from the U.S.A. and Canada, there are small Quaker groups in Mexico, Cuba, and Jamaica. These result from missions work and other contacts by American Friends. Cuba Yearly Meeting was established in 1927, and Jamaica Yearly Meeting in 1941. There are also American Friends' mission stations in Alaska, Bolivia, El Salvador, Guatemala, and Honduras. Soon after the second World War there was a small migration of Friends from the U.S.A. to Costa Rica.

Finally, in Africa, there is a small and scattered Southern Africa Yearly Meeting. In Madagascar there is a long tradition of Friends working together with other Protestants; the outcome may well be a united, independent Malagasy Church with a varying emphasis on distinctively Quaker testimonies. In Kenya, the three American Friends who walked up the rolling hills into the northern part of Nyanza Province in 1903 started what has now become the largest Yearly Meeting in the world, with an adult membership of over 28,000. Someone ought to write a book on this work in Kenya with its present rapid development and its exciting possibilities for the future: on the flowering of Christian character in African Quakers, and on the growing brotherhood of tribes, races, nationalities, and religious denominations, in healing the wounds of recent troubles and age-old ignorance.

CHRISTIAN UNITY

It has been truly said that 'one of the greatest causes of weakness in the testimony of the Church as a whole to the reality of God and the spiritual world, is found in its divisions'.[1]

Christendom is torn asunder, into Catholic, Protestant, and Orthodox, and subdivided into sects that think very ill of one another. These divisions on points of doctrine and practice are among the main reasons why the masses do not believe in Christianity. Spiritual unity has already been sought many times; and Quakers are very likely to have an important part to play in finding it, for, according to them, it is quite impossible to unite Churches on a basis of a common creed and a minimal uniformity in religious practice. 'Christian unity consists, not in *uniformity* of creeds and practices, but in a *common spirit* of loyalty to Jesus Christ, based on a common experience of His power in our souls.'[2] Quaker methods destroy the causes of doctrinal divisions. An unprogrammed meeting allows all Christians to sit down and worship together in the great brotherhood of

[1] See Grubb, op. cit., pp. 211–12.   [2] Ibid., p. 212.

silence. 'The best contribution we can make to Unity among Christians is to stand firmly by our own principles—not, of course, in a contentious spirit—and not to give way on certain points for the sake of a superficial uniformity.' Quakerism must show that it possesses what is real in Christianity, without necessarily having the traditional forms. As a London Yearly Meeting report put it in 1917:

It is as if, all this time, Christendom had been striving to build for itself a body out of a heap of scattered bones, and had thought that the only way to do it was to try by cutting and sawing to make all the bones exactly the same shape and size. Whereas the world is now beginning to see that if only the Spirit of Life were blowing with sufficient strength to make these bones live, then every point of difference whether great or small would reveal itself as no mistake, but rather as the divinely ordered adjustment to the function in the living body that each particular bone was intended to perform. . . . The unity of Christendom is not in our judgement something that needs to be artificially created; it is already here, and only needs to be recognized and acted on.

Although Friends are numerically weak, they are trying to help to bring Christians, and consequently Churches, together, and thus be reconcilers and peace-makers. Because of the doctrinal test imposed by the World Council of Churches, several Quaker Yearly Meetings were unable to take part in the Conferences at Amsterdam (1948) and Lund, Sweden (1952), except as 'observers'. A Quaker meeting on a basis of silent worship was held at both these conferences and was said to have made a deep impression on many of the delegates.

French Friends in 1945 declared that 'diversity of experience and emphasis does not weaken, but enriches, human life'.

CONCLUSION

Several questions may suggest themselves to the reader at this point:

1. What is the religious value of Quakerism in the world today, when moral values have been undermined by a gospel of materialism?

2. In a world in which individual liberty is being eroded more and more every day, even in those countries that proclaim it as a fixed dogma, and in which liberty of thought is dispensed with as a nuisance to the men who happen to be in power, can we still speak of the Seed of God in every man?

3. Can we still preach Christ, when men in all countries bow down in fear before other men or before matter in a state of nuclear fission, or else meet the most appalling catastrophes with brutish apathy?

In the face of such agonizing problems, Friends are still convinced of the Truth given to them by God, believing that along with many others they represent a power for good—a power of active resistance and peace-making. There are still many forms of slavery to be abolished, particularly on the social side of life; many reforms are needed in the field of crime and delinquency; and there is many a fight to be fought against untruth that is in the pay of the press, radio, and television. There have never been so many ways given to man for quickly finding out the truth; and there have never been so many lies! The Quakers, who have seen in the teaching of Christ a Spirit and a way of life rather than a doctrinal 'religion', and who think that this Spirit and this way of life touch every human problem, believe in all humility that they must obey their Light and go on working with all men of goodwill, whether they are church members or are seeking spiritual truth on their own.

Before writing this short study, we had once again read Fox's *Journal* in the French translation by Wilfred Monod (he was not a Quaker), and this sentence caught the eye: 'On peut affirmer sans absurdité que Georges Fox, dans l'avenir, sera béni comme l'un des conducteurs prédestinés du genre humain.' ('It would not be absurd to say that George Fox will come to be revered as one of the men who was called to lead the human race.')

Anthology

TRUTH

Take heed of printing anything more than ye are required of the Lord God.

Nor none stop writing or speaking when ye are moved with the Spirit of the Lord God.

GEORGE FOX (1624–91), *Epistles* (1698) *104*, p. 85.

S. Chinn drew on his imagination for this and another portrait of George Fox, about a hundred years ago.

It is not opinion, or speculation, or notions of what is true, or assent to or the subscription of articles or propositions, though never so soundly worded, that . . . makes a man a true believer or a true Christian. But it is conformity of mind and practice to the will of God, in all holiness of conversation [conduct], according to the dictates of this Divine principle of Light and Life in the soul which denotes a person truly a child of God.

WILLIAM PENN (1644–1718), *A Key . . .* (1692),
from *Works*, 1726 ed., vol. II, p. 781

Sylvanus Bevan, a Quaker apothecary, made three little ivory carvings in high relief of William Penn, about the year 1718. This drawing may be of the one that was carved for Lord Cobham, soon after Penn's death.

After our long seeking the Lord appeared to us, and . . .
brought us by his power to know and see perfectly that God had
given to us, everyone of us in particular, a Light from himself
shining in our hearts and consciences.

> EDWARD BURROUGH (1633–63), Preface to
> *The Great Mistery* (1659)

And this I witness to all the sons of men, that the knowledge
of eternal life I came not to by the letter of the Scripture nor
hearing men speak of the Name of God. I came to the true
knowledge of the Scripture and the eternal rest . . . by the
inspiration of the Spirit of Jesus Christ.

> WILLIAM DEWSBURY (1621–88), *Works* (1689), p. 54

Now is the Day of Beauty broken forth nigh you, even in you.
Yea, Glad Tidings are come unto your wearied souls, by which
a pure Love is begotten in you. The everlasting Truth has been
declared among you, and has reached the witness for God in
your Consciences; and it is sealed upon your hearts and has
become your Teacher.

> JAMES PARNELL (1636–55), written during his
> imprisonment in Colchester Castle

Not by strength of arguments or by a particular disquisition
of each doctrine and convincement of my understanding thereby
came [I] to receive and bear witness of the Truth, but by being
secretly reached by [the] Life.

> ROBERT BARCLAY (1648–90), *Apology* (1678),
> Proposition xi, sect. 7, p. 252

Glory to God forever! who hath chosen us a first-fruits to
himself in this day wherein he is arisen to plead with the nations,
and therefore hath sent us forth to preach this everlasting gospel
unto all—Christ nigh to all, the light in all, the seed sown in the
hearts of all—that men may come and apply their minds to it.

> Ibid., v and vi, sect. 24, p. 123

Seeing no man knoweth the Father but the Son, and he to whom the Son revealeth him; and seeing the revelation of the Son is in and by the Spirit; therefore the testimony of the Spirit is that alone by which the true knowledge of God hath been, is, and can be only revealed. . . . Moreover, these divine inward revelations, which we make absolutely necessary for the building up of true faith, neither do nor can ever contradict the outward testimony of the Scriptures, or right and sound reason.

Ibid., ii, sect. 1, p. 3

The principal rule of Christians under the gospel is not an outward letter, nor law outwardly written and delivered, but an inward spiritual law, engraven in the heart, the law of the Spirit of life, the word that is nigh in the heart and in the mouth.

But the letter of the Scripture is outward, of itself a dead thing, a mere declaration of good things, but not the things themselves;

Therefore it is not, nor can be, the chief or principal rule of Christians. . . .

We shall also be very willing to admit it as a positive certain maxim, That whatsoever any do pretending to the Spirit, which is contrary to the Scriptures, be accounted and reckoned a

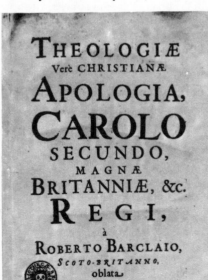

Title-page of the original edition of Barclay's Apology.

delusion of the devil. For as we never lay claim to the Spirit's leadings, that we may cover ourselves in anything that is evil; so we know, that as every evil contradicts the Scriptures, so it doth also the Spirit in the first place, from which the Scriptures came, and whose motions can never contradict one another, though they may appear sometimes to be contradictory to the blind eye of the natural man, as Paul and James seem to contradict one another.

Ibid., iii, sects. 2 and 6, pp. 46 and 55

Deep within us all there is an amazing inner sanctuary of the soul, a holy place, a Divine Centre, a speaking Voice, to which we may continuously return. Eternity is at our hearts, pressing upon our time-torn lives, warming us with intimations of an astounding destiny, calling us home unto Itself. Yielding to these persuasions, gladly committing ourselves in body and soul, utterly and completely, to the Light Within, is the beginning of true life. It is a dynamic centre, a creative Life that presses to birth within us. . . . It is a seed stirring to life if we do not choke it. . . . Here is the Slumbering Christ, stirring to be awakened, to become the soul we clothe in earthly form and action. And He is within us all. . . .

For though we begin the practice of secret prayer with a strong sense that we are the initiators and that by our wills we are establishing our habits, maturing experience brings awareness of being met, and tutored, purged and disciplined, simplified and made pliant in His holy will by a power waiting within us. For God Himself works in our souls, in their deepest depths, taking increasing control as we are progressively willing to be prepared for His wonder.

Thomas R. Kelly (1893–1941),
A Testament of Devotion, 1941, pp. 29 and 41

The Quakers did not apply to the sacrifice of Christ the Old Testament concept of a blood sacrifice offered to appease an angry God. The blood sacrifice commanded by the Mosaic law was for them an external form belonging to the old dispensation.

They believed that the word 'blood' was used metaphorically in the New Testament as a figure of speech natural in view of the cultural background of the Hebrew people, but not one which could have the same meaning for themselves. They more characteristically considered the 'Blood of Christ' to be the Light Within in its redeeming and sanctifying capacity.

George Fox in 1648 writes at the beginning of his ministry:

> Soon after there was another great meeting of professors, and a captain, whose name was Amor Stoddard, came in. And they were discoursing of the blood of Christ; and as they were discoursing of it, I saw, through the immediate opening of the invisible Spirit, the blood of Christ. And I cried out among them, and said, 'Do ye not see the blood of Christ? see it in your hearts, to sprinkle your hearts and consciences from dead works to serve the living God?' for I saw it, the blood of the New Covenant, how it came into the heart. This startled the professors, who would have the blood only without them and not in them (p. 23).

This is the usual Quaker emphasis on the inward life rather than the outward event.

HOWARD BRINTON, *Friends for 300 Years*, pp. 41 and 42

WORSHIP AND SPIRITUAL EXPERIENCES

All Friends, everywhere, keep your meetings waiting in the light, which from the Lord Jesus Christ doth come; so will you receive power from Him, and have the refreshing springs of life opened to your souls, and be kept sensible of the tender mercies of the Lord. And know one another in the life (ye that be turned to the light) and in the power, which comes from the Lord Jesus Christ.

GEORGE FOX (1624–91), *Epistle 105*, p. 86

The Lord of heaven and earth we found to be near at hand, and, as we waited upon Him in pure silence, our minds out of all things, His heavenly presence appeared in our assemblies, when there was no language, tongue nor speech from any creature. The Kingdom of heaven did gather us and catch us all, as in a net, and His heavenly power at one time drew many hundreds to land. We came to know a place to stand in and what to wait in; and the Lord appeared daily to us, to our astonishment, amazement and great admiration. . . .

And from that day forward, our hearts were knit unto the Lord and one unto another in true and fervent love, in the covenant of Life with God; and that was as a strong bond upon all our spirits, which united us one unto another. We met together in the unity of the Spirit, and of the bond of peace treading down under our feet all reasoning about religion.

> FRANCIS HOWGILL (1618–68), *Christian Discipline of the Religious Society of Friends in Great Britain*, 1922, reprint 1945 (hereafter referred to as *English Discipline*, to distinguish it from the parallel volumes issued in Philadelphia), Part I, p. 18; being abridged from the testimony of Francis Howgill (1618–68) at the beginning of the *Works* of Edward Burroughs (1672)

Oh, how may I do to set forth the fullness of God's love to our souls. No tongue can express it; no heart can conceive it; no mind can comprehend it. O the ravishment, the raptures, the glorious bright-shining countenance of the Lord our God; which is our fullness in emptiness, our strength in weakness, our health in sickness, our life in death, our joy in sorrow, our peace in disquietness, our praise in heaviness, our power in all needs and necessities. He alone is a full God unto us, and to all that can trust in Him. He hath emptied us of ourselves, and hath unbottomed us of ourselves; and hath wholly built us upon the sure foundation, the Rock of Ages, Christ Jesus the Light of the world. . . . As being members of one body, Christ Jesus being our Head, we must needs suffer together that we may rejoice together. A true sorrow begets a true joy; a true cross, a true crown. . . . The deeper the sorrow, the greater the joy; the heavier the cross, the weightier the crown.

> KATHARINE EVANS (d. 1692), *English Discipline*,
> Part I, p. 25. From letters to her husband

At last, after all my distresses, wanderings and sore travels, I met with some writings of this people called Quakers, which I cast a slight eye upon and disdained, as falling very short of that wisdom, light, life and power, which I had been longing for and searching after. . . . After a long time, I was invited to hear one of them, as I had been often, they in tender love pitying me and feeling my want of that which they possessed. . . .

When I came, I felt the presence and power of the Most High among them, and words of truth from the Spirit of truth reaching to my heart and conscience, opening my state as in the presence of the Lord. Yea, I did not only feel words and demonstrations from without, but I felt the dead quickened, the seed raised, insomuch as my heart, in the certainty of light and clearness of true sense, said, 'This is He; this is He; there is no other; this is He whom I have waited for and sought after from my childhood, who was always near me, and had often begotten life in my heart, but I knew Him not distinctly, nor how to receive Him or dwell with Him.' And then in this sense, in the melting and breakings of my spirit, was I given up to the Lord, to become His, both in waiting for the further revealing of His seed in me, and to serve Him in the life and power of His seed.

ISAAC PENINGTON (1616–79), *English Discipline*, Part I, pp. 27 and 28

When we came to the meeting [at Broughton, Cumberland], being a little late, it was full gathered, and I went among the throng of the people on the forms, and sat still among them in that inward condition and mental retirement. . . .

For, not long after I had sat down among them, that heavenly and watery cloud overshadowing my mind brake into a sweet abounding shower of celestial rain, and the greatest part of the meeting was broken together, dissolved and comforted in the same divine and holy presence and influence of the true, holy and heavenly Lord, which was divers times repeated before the meeting ended. . . .

Our joy was mutual and full, though in the efflux of many tears. . . .

my noticing it, till my brother, speaking to me, drew my attention, and I saw that we two only were left in the house.

STEPHEN GRELLET (1773–1855), *Memoirs*,
ed. Seebohm (1860), pp. 24–25

When the souls of many sitting in silence are being oriented together the effect of the communion may be felt. The souls are in chorus if the voices are not. Each spirit collects itself . . . gathering the disturbed consciousness to one point, inwards to the trysting place with the Eternal. . . . We take stock spiritually—throw away the rubbish, check our estimates, and gain

The meeting being ended, the Peace of God . . . remained as a holy canopy over my mind in a silence out of the reach of all words, and where no idea but the Word Himself can be conceived.

THOMAS STORY (1670–1742), *English Discipline*,
Part I, pp. 36 and 37

[A twenty-two-year-old French refugee at a Friends' Meeting on Long Island, New York, in 1795.]

It was a memorable meeting—held in silence, however, as usual—never to be forgotten. Very soon after sitting down, great was the awfulness and the reverence that came upon me. It was succeeded by such a view and sense of my sinful life that I was like one crushed under the millstones. . . . But how can I set forth the fulness of heavenly joy that filled me when the hope was again raised that there was One, even He whom I had pierced, Jesus Christ the Redeemer, that was able to save me. . . .

. . . The meeting concluded, and the people retired, without

Stephen Grellet.

peace at the end, it may be after stiff conflict with the natural man. . . . Often humility and penitence cover the whole man. We make contact each for himself with the Real and the Eternal, and thereby gain strength over temptation and sin. In the distractions of daily life, in the crowded multiplicity of detail, we may fail to see the wood for the trees. Here we are able to look at ourselves and to look from ourselves. How superficial is the view that in silence there is nothing going on. This is what Friends call a living silence.

JOHN W. GRAHAM (1859–1932), *The Faith of a Quaker* (1920), pp. 241–2

On one never-to-be-forgotten Sunday morning, I found myself one of a small company of silent worshippers, who were content to sit down together without words, that each might feel after and draw near to the Divine Presence, unhindered at least, if not helped, by any human utterance. . . . My whole soul was filled with the unutterable peace of the undisturbed opportunity

The interior of Arch Street meeting-house, Philadelphia.

for communion with God, with the sense that at last I had found a place where I might, without the faintest suspicion of insincerity, join with others in simply seeking His presence.

CAROLINE E. STEPHEN (1835–1909), *Quaker Strongholds*, 1923 edition, pp. 2–4

Silent worship seems to Friends to be their natural method. It is healing; it is uniting; it cleanses, challenges, stimulates. It helps us to get down to those deeper currents of the soul that are so often neglected in life's hurry and bustle; it enables us to centre down into fellowship with the Eternal and to hear the still small voice of God. . . .

May we never forget that our public worship is a corporate act: we meet, not as isolated individuals, but as a group. In the silence we enter into fellowship not only with God, but with one another. . . . Such a meeting will indeed be a communion service.

No wonder then that worship in this sense is often said to be the Quaker's sacrament! . . . Suddenly or gradually we realise 'the Presence in the midst', and the silence becomes fully sacramental. Thus comes the sense of our communion one with another through partaking together of the Bread of Life, and we go forth to actualise that communion and fellowship in our daily lives.

GERALD K. HIBBERT (1872–1957), *Quaker Fundamentals*, pp. 5 and 6

At first sight, it might appear that the meeting can only be described by negatives—there is no altar, no liturgy, no pulpit, no sermon, no organ, no choir, no sacrament, and no person in authority. No external object of attention prevents the worshipper from turning inward and there finding the revelation of the divine Will. Whatever is outward in worship must come as a direct result of what is inward—otherwise, it will be form without power. There must first be withdrawal to the source of power and then a return with power.

HOWARD BRINTON, *Friends for 300 Years*, p. 63

We must take into account both the influence of the spoken word and the feeling of presence and light that each worshipper radiates. Those who speak rarely if at all in Meeting are just as indispensable for creating this atmosphere of quiet worship. We know by experience all that is contributed by mere presence of some one man or woman. Such riches are inaccessible to solitary worship and even to liturgical worship, for in the latter there is no individual activity; those present have walking-on parts to play; they are not actors as in Quaker worship.

> HENRY VAN ETTEN, *Le culte Quaker d'après les données de la mystique* (1945)

THE SACRAMENTS

For he set up in the church one faith, which Christ was the author of; and one baptism, which was that of the Spirit, into the one body; and one Lord Jesus Christ, the spiritual baptizer, who John said should come after him. . . .

You must have fellowship in Christ in his sufferings: if ye will reign with him, ye must suffer with him; if ye will live with him, ye must die with him; and if ye die with him, ye must be buried with him: and being buried with him in the true baptism ye also rise with him. Then having suffered with him, died with him, and been buried with him, if ye are risen with Christ, 'seek those things which are above, where Christ sitteth on the right hand of God'. Eat the bread which comes from above, which is not outward bread; and drink the cup of salvation which he gives in his kingdom, which is not outward wine. And then there will not be a looking at the things that are seen (as outward bread and wine, and water are:) for, as says the apostle, 'The things that are seen are temporal, but the things that are not seen are eternal.'

> GEORGE FOX (1624–91), *Journal*, Bi-centenary ed., vol. I, pp. 340 and 342

A French exile in London, 1727, visits an English Quaker, Andrew Pitt

I began with the question that good French Catholics have more than once put to the Protestants. 'My dear sir,' I said, 'are you baptized?'

'No,' replied the Quaker, 'nor are the other Friends.'

''Sdeath!' I retorted, 'are you not Christians then?'

'My son,' he answered, in a gentle tone, 'swear not. We are Christians, and endeavour to be *good* Christians; but we do not think that Christianity consists of throwing cold water over someone's head, with a little salt.'

'Well, by God,' I retorted, stung by this blasphemy, 'have you forgotten then that Jesus Christ was baptized by John?'

'Friend, again I tell thee; swear not,' said the kindly Quaker. 'Christ received the baptism of John, but he himself never baptized anyone. We are not the followers of John, but of Christ.'

'Alack!' I said, 'how you would be burnt at the stake in countries where the Inquisition is, you poor fellow!'

VOLTAIRE (1694–1778), from 'Première Lettre sur les Quakers', in *Lettres Philosophiques*

'There are not merely two or seven sacraments, but seventy times seven, for him whose heart seeks ever fellowship with his brothers and with the Father above him. . . . The error of the sacramentalist in the past has often rather been that he has confined the Divine presence and the Divine working to certain fixed channels and unchanging visible signs. We who hold that these good men have narrowed down the freedom of the inner life need to meet them not by denying the Divine presence where they see it, but by trying to see and to realise that presence ourselves more fully throughout all our lives.'

T. EDMUND HARVEY (1876–1955), *A Wayfarer's Faith* (1913), pp. 57, 62

. . . may it not be wise to dispense with the ceremony entirely? I believe it is—though for my own part I would never try to draw anyone away from sharing in the Communion service if he finds that by so doing he gains a deeper consciousness of fellowship with Christ. There is a real and important place in the Church of Christ for those who can prove that their union with Him is independent of such outward aids.

On the whole my judgment is clear that we are right in dispensing with water Baptism, and with the celebration of the Lord's Supper—provided we make more, and not less, of the realities for which they stand, and seek to weave them into all our life. Can we find, like the early Christians, that our ordinary meals are true eucharists? Let us use eagerly the silent pause for thanksgiving with which we have been taught to begin them, but which it is to be feared is too often formal or neglected. Stephen Grellet once said, near the end of his life, that, since his conversion to Christianity, he did not remember that he had ever taken a meal without thinking of the broken body and the shed blood of his Lord. Was not he a Sacramentalist in the real sense?

EDWARD GRUBB (1854–1939), *What is Quakerism?* (1917), pp. 86–7

We can appeal to the Gospel according to John, which was called by Clement of Alexandria the 'spiritual Gospel'. John is not discussing ceremonies: for him everything is spiritual and symbolical. Christ is the Bread, the Shepherd, the Door, the Way, the Vine. No rite is mentioned—although many details are given of Christ's last meal with his disciples —with the exception of the command 'Ye also ought to wash one another's feet.' That command is definite enough; but Christians agree to interpret it spiritually. . . . The Churches do not of course agree on the sacrament of communion; and it is not for us to discuss the views of the different Christian Churches on this subject.

Edward Grubb.

. . . Our meetings of silent worship are often worthy to be called communion meals, taken together round an invisible table with our Master at the head. . . . The same is true when a child is born, and is presented to God by his parents in the presence of the Meeting (*Ecclesia*) solemnly gathered together: this can be an opportunity for spiritual enrichment and reach the true meaning of sacrament: 'an outward and visible sign of an inward and spiritual grace'. Marriages and funerals must also be opportunities for consecration and blessing for the whole Meeting. All life can and must be sacramental.

HENRY VAN ETTEN, *Le Quakerisme*, 1953

UNITY

How sweet and pleasant is it to the truly spiritual eye to see several sorts of believers, several forms of Christians in the school of Christ, every one learning their own lesson, performing their own peculiar service, and knowing, owning and loving one another in their several places and different performances to their Master, to whom they are to give an account, and not to quarrel with one another about their different practices. For this is the true ground of love and unity, not that such a man walks and does just as I do, but because I feel the same spirit and life in him.

ISAAC PENINGTON (1616–79), *English Discipline*,
Part II, p. 95

The humble, meek, merciful, just, pious and devout souls are everywhere of one religion; and when death has taken off the mask, they will know one another though the divers liveries they wear here makes them strangers.

WILLIAM PENN (1644–1718), *Some Fruits of Solitude*,
Part I, No. 519

The unity of Christians never did nor ever will or can stand in uniformity of thought or opinion, but in Christian love only.

THOMAS STORY (1670–1742),
Discourse at Horslydown, 1737

All Christians can sit down together in the fellowship of silence, if they choose to do so, and give freedom to any to speak or offer vocal prayer as they are led by the Spirit. I believe it may be said with truth that the Quaker method of worship is the only one in which all Christians can join without difficulties arising.

> EDWARD GRUBB (1854–1939), *What is Quakerism?*
> (1917), p. 213

The disciples of Christ are found in all denominations. The denominations differ just as the disciples differed as to their characters and temperaments; but they form a fellowship beyond all limits of their nature. This unity must be recognized today, in a time of desertion and struggle, which sometimes seems to be fought rather for the sake of outward forms than of essentials. It is not organization that matters, but the Light which is potent to dissolve organizations and to re-shape them.

> ALFONS PAQUET (1881–1944), *Wohin führt uns
> Jesus Christus*, pp. 15–16

The existence of our Society as a separate member of the Christian community is due to our belief that in this way we can best testify to that aspect of the Truth which has been shown to us. But when those who are followers of the Lord Jesus Christ try in simplicity to carry out His will, we believe that unity will be found beyond the diversity.

This trust is one that we can neither take up nor lay down at pleasure.

> ALFONS PAQUET, *English Discipline*, Part II, p. 96

Yet still more astonishing is the Holy Fellowship, the Blessed Community, to those who are within it. . . .

In the Fellowship cultural and educational and national and racial differences are levelled. Unlettered men are at ease with the truly humble scholar who lives in the Life, and the scholar listens with joy and openness to the precious experiences of

God's dealing with the working man. . . . We overleap the boundaries of church membership and find Lutherans and Roman Catholics, Jews and Christians, within the Fellowship. . . . Particularly does devotional literature become illuminated, for the *Imitation of Christ*, and Augustine's *Confessions*, and Brother Lawrence's *Practice of the Presence of God* speak the language of the souls who live at the Centre. Time telescopes and vanishes, centuries and creeds are overleaped. . . .

And this fellowship is deeper than democracy, conceived as an ideal of group living. It is a theocracy, wherein God rules and guides and directs His listening children. The centre of authority is not in man, not in the group, but in the creative God Himself.

THOMAS R. KELLY (1893–1941), *A Testament of Devotion* (1941), pp. 81–84

The Quaker Star—symbol of Friends' relief work—at Fresnes Prison; Friends worked there 1941–6.

RELIGION

The Gospel religion is very precious, being inwardly felt and experienced in the life and power of it; but a bare profession of it, out of the life and power of godliness, is of no value in the sight of God, nor is it of any profit or advantage to the soul.

ISAAC PENINGTON (1616–79), *Works*, 1681 ed.,
Part II, p. 496

We claim to be a people who have found rest in God; a people building our house upon the rock, through obedience to those 'words of eternal life' given forth by Christ, the Word. We recognise His Voice as speaking to us, not only in the pages of Scripture, but also in the whole course of life as ordered by Him; and yet more closely in the inmost chamber of our own hearts; and we desire to yield to it an undivided allegiance.

CAROLINE E. STEPHEN (1835–1909),
Quaker Strongholds, 4th ed., 1907, p. 160

Religion is not a matter of form, but of the very life.

ROBERT SPENCE WATSON (1837–1911), Address
at the Manchester Conference, 1895, p. 140

. . . the religious life is the inward life of the spirit. But no place or time can limit its action, nor any symbol adequately express it, and that therefore of necessity no priest can claim to intervene between that inward life and its source of strength and power.

To the soul that feeds upon the bread of life the outward conventions of religion are no longer needful. Hid with Christ in God, there is for him small place for outward rites, for all experience is a holy baptism, a perpetual supper with the Lord, and all life a sacrifice, holy and acceptable unto God. This hidden life, this inward vision, this immediate and intimate union between the soul and God, this, as revealed in Jesus Christ, is the basis of the Quaker faith.

JOHN WILHELM ROWNTREE (1868–1905),
Essays and Addresses, pp. 100, 92

The affirmation that life is *one* and religious throughout . . . is our first general principle.

For the Quaker the whole of life should be seen and understood on the religious plane; life must be sacramental, and we should not separate its various spheres, as we are so prone to do. This is an absolute difficult of attainment; but for us this absolute represents the ultimate truth. For God, the life which he has created as a manifold thing can have but different aspects, facets of one diamond reflecting the light. So our second principle will be that *fundamentally* there is no distinction between spiritual work and material work. In *our* eyes, possibly, one may be higher than the other, but really they are only two sides of the same thing. For man, to pray is spiritual and to act is material; but for God there are not these distinctions, especially in the case of a 'material' work required by Him and through which His Will and Love may express themselves. Worship is at once the highest manifestation of our religious life and the starting point of our activities, and hence to work without praying is a great error, just as to pray without working is far from the way followed by Christ on earth: pure contemplation was not his method.

HENRY VAN ETTEN, *Ouvriers avec Dieu*, Paris, 1944

Men who are free in God have no call to live in 'fear and trembling', for they have their witness to give. If every follower of Christ had within him his own cathedral, he would not be shocked at the demolition of places of worship, such as has taken place in Russia and elsewhere; his regrets would be on an artistic and cultural level; but his inward church would be unaffected. . . . Every one who is struggling for the emancipation of the soul, mind and body of man is of a Christian spirit, even if he denies it. All movements and societies working for the reconciliation of men, are of God and therefore of Truth, and therefore are with us and not against us.

HENRY VAN ETTEN, *Le Quaker en face des problèmes de la vie*, 1932

Let us be quite clear that mystical exaltations are not essential to religious dedication. . . . Many a man professes to be without a shred of mystical elevation, yet is fundamentally a heaven-dedicated soul. It would be a tragic mistake to suppose that religion is only for a small group, who have certain vivid but transient inner experiences, and to preach those experiences so that those who are relatively insensitive to them should feel excluded, denied access to the Eternal love, deprived of a basic necessity for religious living. The crux of religious living lies in the *will*, not in transient and variable states. Utter dedication of will to God is open to *all*. . . . Where the will to will God's will is present, there is a child of God. When there are graciously given to us such glimpses of glory as aid us in softening own-will, then we may be humbly grateful. But glad willing away of self that the will of God, so far as it can be discerned, may become what we will—that is the basic condition.

THOMAS R. KELLY (1893–1941), *The Gathered Meeting*, pp. 13–14

SIMPLICITY

O that we who declare against wars, and acknowledge our trust to be in God only, may walk in the light, and therein examine our foundation and motives in holding great estates! May we look upon our treasures, the furniture of our houses, and our garments, and try whether the seeds of war have nourishment in these our possessions.

JOHN WOOLMAN (1720–72), *Journal*, New Century ed. (1900), p. 279

Christianity is tested, not only in the shop and in the office, but also in the home. In the standard of living adopted by the home-makers, in the portion of income devoted to comforts, recreations and luxuries, in willingness to be content with simplicity, the members of a household, both older and younger, may bear witness that there is a Way of Life that does not depend on the abundance of the things possessed.

From London Yearly Meeting *Epistle*, 1911

Life from the Centre is a life of unhurried peace and power. It is simple. It is serene. It is amazing. It is triumphant. It is radiant. It takes no time, but it occupies all our time. And it makes our life programmes new and overcoming. We need not get frantic. He is at the helm. And when our little day is done we lie down quietly in peace, for all is well.

THOMAS R. KELLY (1893–1941), *A Testament of Devotion* (1941), p. 124

Carefully maintain in your own conduct and encourage in your families truthfulness and sincerity. In your style of living, in your dress and in the furniture of your houses, choose what is simple and beautiful. Encourage the reading of good books, so that the taste thus formed may instinctively reject the trivial and the base.

General Advices of London Yearly Meeting, 1928

THE RELIGIOUS EDUCATION OF YOUNG CHILDREN

Our belief in the divine spark in each individual person involves complete respect for the soul of a child: he belongs to himself even before belonging to his parents, from whom he is often different in temperament, tastes and abilities. The most important duty facing parents who take religion seriously is to hand on to their children those things that they hold to be true and good. . . . They must remember that this education must be as liberal and undogmatic as possible, if it is to be worth-while and to respect the conscience of the child. Such education will be most fruitful if it is given in the family and by the parents themselves, whose character and behaviour within the family circle have a very great influence on the children, who in their turn naturally have complete confidence in them. . . . Respecting a child's liberty does not mean that we must let him flounder unaided amongst the problems that he will probably have to face in the future. He must be provided, step by step, with the material aids that are indispensable for spiritual growth, particularly books (suitable to his age) based on the Bible or the New Testament, or the actual text of the Bible.

As early as possible, children should be taught to pray, speaking to God quite naturally and in their ordinary language. . . . Religious education, having started at home, should at an early age be complemented and deepened by children's meetings, so as to establish the human contacts that are essential to education; these meetings should be led by a qualified person who will at the same time be able to advise and help those parents who do not feel they are equal to their task.

> From *L'Education Religieuse des Enfants*,
> France Yearly Meeting, Paris, 1943

INTERNATIONAL RELATIONS

Through the dark cloud of selfishness and materialism, shines the Eternal Light of the Christ in man. It can never perish. This light of Christ in the heart of every man is the ground of our hope, the basis of our faith in the spiritual unity of all races and all nations. . . .

We stretch out our hands in fellowship, sympathy and love across frontiers, lands and seas. We call upon all men everywhere to unite in the service of healing the broken world, to bear one another's burdens, and so fulfil the Law of Christ.

> *A Message to all Men.* Issued by Meeting for
> Sufferings, London, 1919

Instead of self-seeking we must put sacrifice; instead of domination, co-operation. Fear and suspicion must give place to trust and the spirit of understanding . . . and thus to make all humanity a society of friends.

> Message of the Friends' World Conference, London, 1920

Therefore to Friends and to men and women of all nations we dare to say: Turn from the way of strife; admit the power of God into your lives, nor be dismayed at all.

> From the *Epistle* from London Yearly Meeting, May 1939

The Christian faith, which we believe is the hope of our troubled world, is a revolutionary faith. . . . We rejoice in the movements, appearing in many parts of the world at once, which are inspired by the desire for social justice, equal rights for all races and the dignity of the individual person. These changes can neither be achieved nor prevented by war. War leads to a vicious circle of hatred, oppression, subversive movements, false propaganda, rearmament, and new wars. . . .

Let us join together throughout the world to grow more food, to heal and prevent disease, to conserve and develop the resources of the good earth to the glory of God and the comfort of man's distress. These are among the tasks to which, in humility for our share in the world's shame, and in faith in the power of love, we call our own Society and all men and nations everywhere.

Message of Friends' World Conference, Oxford, 1952

It is true for us . . . that spiritual guidance and silent worship practised corporately . . . carry us on to a deep communion of spirit, wherein is determined our way of conducting all our corporate affairs. Quaker method, like our worship and our ministry, and our whole way of life, derives from Quaker doctrine.

As with all Christian people, our understanding of the nature of God centres in the person of Christ. For He is our Light. In Him we see and understand the working of the Love of God. In our thought we identify His Spirit with the inward illumination which comes to the pure in heart. He saves men by the redemptive power of the communion of His love.

All these thoughts deeply influence and determine the nature of our international work. The Society of Friends is not resting on a theological dogma, an institutional conception of the church, or a biblical literalism. It rests on an inward experience of the soul, the working power of which it has long proved. It invites men to this experience and the way of life that follows from it. This is the primary purpose of its international service. In the midst of war it invites men to taste of the peaceable spirit which pertains to this experience; and in the midst of 'peace' it

Title page of William Penn's Essay, 1693

AN
ESSAY

Towards the Present and Future

PEACE

OF

Europe,

BY THE

Establishment of an *European*

Dyet, Parliament,

Or Estates.

Beati Pacifici.

Cedant Arma Togæ.

London, Printed in the Year, 1693.

W. Penn.

brings to men this zest of spiritual overcoming, having faith to seek in all men the seed of divine life.

> CARL HEATH (1869–1950), *Quaker Thought in International Service*, (1921), p. 6 (One sentence altered, with permission.)

SCIENCE AND RELIGION

I dare say that most of you are by no means reluctant to accept the scientific epic of the Creation, holding it perhaps as more to the glory of God than the traditional story. . . .

Probably most astronomers, if they were to speak frankly, would confess to some chafing when they are reminded of the psalm 'The heavens declare the glory of God'. . . . There is another passage from the Old Testament that comes nearer to my own sympathies: 'And, behold, the Lord passed by, and a great and strong wind rent the mountains, and brake in pieces the rocks before the Lord; but the Lord was not in the wind: and after the wind an earthquake; but the Lord was not in the earthquake: and after the earthquake a fire; but the Lord was not in the fire: and after the fire a still small voice. . . . And behold there came a voice unto him, and said, What doest thou here, Elijah?' (I Kings 19: 11–13).

Wind, earthquake, fire—meteorology, seismology, physics—pass in review, as we have been reviewing the natural forces of evolution; the Lord was not in them. Afterwards, a stirring, an awakening in the organ of the brain, a voice which asks 'What doest thou here?' . . .

In comparing the certainty of things spiritual and things temporal, let us not forget this—Mind is the first and most direct thing in our experience; all else is remote inference.

That environment of space and time and matter, of light and colour and concrete things, which seems so vividly real to us, is probed deeply by every device of physical science and at the bottom we reach symbols. Its substance has melted into shadow.

'Is the unseen world revealed by the mystical outlook a reality?' Reality is one of those indeterminate words which might lead to infinite philosophical discussions and irrelevancies.

There is less danger of misunderstanding if we put the question in the form: 'Are we, in pursuing the mystical outlook, facing the hard facts of experience?' Surely we are. I think that those who would wish to take cognizance of nothing but the measurements of the scientific world made by our sense-organs are shirking one of the most immediate facts of experience. . . .

In justifying the place of religious experience in human life, we have not to consider it from the point of view of propagating a creed . . . in speaking of religious experience I do not attempt to prove the existence of religious experience, any more than in lecturing on optics I should attempt to prove the existence of sight. . . .

The crucial point for us is not a conviction of the existence of a supreme God but a conviction of the revelation of a supreme God. I will not speak here of the revelation in a life that was lived nineteen hundred years ago. . . . I confine myself to the revelation implied in the indwelling of the divine spirit in the mind of man. . . .

I would not go so far as to urge that no kind of defence of creeds is possible. But I think it may be said that Quakerism in dispensing with creeds holds out a hand to the scientist.

> ARTHUR S. EDDINGTON (1882–1945), Swarthmore
> Lecture, *Science and the Unseen World*, 1929, pp. 16 ff.

PHILADELPHIA AND PENNSYLVANIA

And thou Philadelphia, the virgin settlement of this province, named before thou wast born, what love, what care, what service, and what travail has there been to bring thee forth and preserve thee from such as would abuse and defile thee!

O that thou mayest be kept from the evil that would overwhelm thee: that, faithful to the God of thy mercies, in the life of righteousness, thou mayest be preserved to the end!

> WILLIAM PENN's farewell message, 1684

. . . I will tell you, without repeating myself, that I love the Quakers. Yes, if the sea did not make me unbearably sick, I would go and finish the rest of my career—if any—in thy heart,

O Pennsylvania. Thou liest on the fortieth parallel of latitude; thy climate is most mild and agreeable; thy lands are fertile, thy houses are roomy, thy habitants are industrious, thy manufactures are held in honour. Eternal peace reigns among thy citizens; crime is almost unknown, and there has only been one example of a man banished from the country. He richly deserved it; he was an Anglican priest who, having turned Quaker, proved unworthy to be one. This wretch was no doubt possessed of the devil, for he dared to preach intolerance; his name was George Keith: he was driven out; I do not know where he went; but may all intolerant people go with him!

VOLTAIRE, Article on 'Quakers' in the
Dictionnaire Philosophique, 1764 onwards

SOME MAXIMS OF WILLIAM PENN AND PIERRE CERESOLE

WILLIAM PENN (1644–1718)

Union of Friends

They that love beyond the world, cannot be separated by it.

Death cannot kill, what never dies.

Nor can spirits ever be divided that love and live in the same Divine Principle; the root and record of their friendship.

If absence be not death, neither is theirs.

Death is but crossing the world, as friends do the seas; they live in one another still.

Education

We are in pain to make them scholars, but not men! To talk, rather than to know, which is true canting.

Children had rather be making of tools and instruments of play; shaping, drawing, framing, and building, etc., than getting some rules of propriety of speech by heart; and those also would follow with more judgment, and less trouble and time.

Pride

He would have others obey him, even his own kind; but he will not obey God, that is so much above him, and who made him.

He is curious to wash, dress and perfume his body, but careless of his soul. The one shall have many hours, the other not so many minutes. This shall have three or four new suits in a year, but that must wear its old cloaths still.

Censoriousness

They have a right to censure, that have a heart to help: the rest is cruelty, not justice.

Simplicity

The most common things are the most useful; which shews both the wisdom and goodness of the great Lord of the family of the world.

Marriage

Men are generally more careful of the breed of their horses and dogs than of their children.

Wherefore use her not as a servant, whom thou would'st, perhaps, have serv'd seven years to have obtained.

Government

Let the people think they govern, and they will be governed. The method cannot fail if those they trust are to be trusted.

Religion

To be furious in religion, is to be irreligiously religious.

It were better to be of no Church, than to be bitter for any.

From *Some Fruits of Solitude*

PIERRE CERESOLE (1879–1945) (from notebooks he kept purely for his own reading)

Truth

Pray the Eternal to keep your weather-vane in good trim so that it readily responds to the true winds of the spirit and doesn't get jammed by the rust of tradition in a position unrelated to the truth or to the true currents of the spirit.

Don't be timid. Remember that all your words, all your expressions of belief are mere approximations and eternally inadequate. The crime is to want to nail everything down in a final way with the authority of the Church or the Bible.

In all seriousness and all humility, put everything to the test, especially religion. It is a matter of life or death.

Sincerity

Consider the glorious but perfectly useless (! ?) flower set in green velvet on some inaccessible ledge of the Alps where no one will ever see it.

A flower that tries to lean over the edge of the precipice so that people down below will notice it is grotesque, is rejected from the kingdom of true and lovely things.

Less bitter to be spat upon by the soldiers than worshipped by the disciples with prudence and moderation.

Education

Speak to a child as if the man you hope to make of him—straightforward, discerning, with an exacting standard of truth and honour—already had his eyes upon you.

Fellowship

Hell is an invention of well-meaning people to get rid of their chief and most awkward duty, which is to come to terms with rogues and restore them into fellowship.

Sacrifice

Sacrifice is the law of life. But not the *taking* of another's life; only the giving of one's own.

Prayer and Action

God is not a personage who orders us to prostrate ourselves before him—a radically false position—but one who says: Stand up; here is my task for you; take it and get on with it.

God does not require incense from us; what he does require is that we should *listen* and *take action*—the true response of love.

God did not stop speaking two thousand years ago. He speaks to you personally today every time an inward voice asks you to do a kind or generous deed or to suffer for the sake of someone else. It is to you personally that God speaks at this moment, and it is *through you* that he speaks when he inspires you to do some service. Be brave enough to listen at first hand to what God says to you.

> From *For Peace and Truth*, translated and edited by
> John W. Harvey and Christina Yates, 1954

A PRAYER

Thou, O Christ, convince us by Thy Spirit; thrill us with Thy Divine passion; drown our selfishness in Thy invading Love; lay on us the burden of the world's suffering; drive us forth with the apostolic fervour of the early Church! So only can our message be delivered. 'Speak to the children of Israel that they go forward.'

> JOHN WILHELM ROWNTREE (1868–1905), speaking at
> the Manchester Conference in 1895

ACKNOWLEDGEMENTS

The translator is grateful to many Friends for help in revising the book; in particular to John Nickalls; to Edward Milligan and Muriel Hicks of the Friends House Library; to Benita Barber of the Home Service Committee; to Cyril Mummery for advice on Chapter I; to Frederick J. Tritton, Howard Brinton and Beatrice Saxon Snell for detailed comments, and to the author for his willing co-operation in the rewriting of the text for an English-reading public.

X X X X PROCLA

LADA BY ORD

SS AND STOW

PHILADA

MDCCLIII

CHRONOLOGICAL TABLE OF EVENTS MENTIONED IN THIS BOOK

(Chapters I–XI)

The bell ordered from an English firm in 1751 to celebrate the jubilee of the second charter of Pennsylvania. It was rung on a dramatic occasion in the War of Independence, and gained the name of Liberty Bell in the agitation over slavery early in the 19th century. The crack was drilled out in the hope of preventing it from spreading.

186

Co-operation: *one of many posters put out by the Friends' organizations in England.*

'*Anno Domini* 1675':

the foundation-stone of Briggflatts meeting-house, Sedbergh, England.

BOOKS FOR FURTHER READING

Quakers have always been more interested in quality of living than in theory or theology. The reader who wishes to explore Quakerism further is unlikely to find any theoretical work, apart from Barclay's *Apology* (1676), that has been widely read by Friends. Many of the books that they find most helpful are accounts of personal experience. Quakerism—which is of course a recent word—turns out to be not so much an 'ism' as a way of life and worship.

Every Friends' Meeting-house maintains a lending library; and books and pamphlets on all aspects of Quakerism may be obtained from:

Friends Book Centre, Euston Road, London, N.W.1.
Friends Book Store, 302 Arch Street, Philadelphia 6, Pa.
The Friends Book and Supply House, 101 Quaker Hill Drive, Richmond, Indiana.

The books listed below were available in London at the end of 1958. Further reading could well begin with the books on faith and practice; London and Philadelphia publish separate versions:

Christian Discipline of the Religious Society of Friends in Great Britain (a new edition of Parts I and II will appear soon)
1. Christian Life, Faith and Thought.
2. Christian Practice.
3. Church Government.

Faith and Practice of the Philadelphia Yearly Meeting of the Religious Society of Friends, 1955
1. Faith and Thought.
2. Practice and Procedure.
3. Quaker Witness to the Faith.

Advices and Queries have been regularly brought before Meetings since the seventeenth century; they have been constantly revised; they are printed in *Church Government* (Part 3 of the English Books of Discipline) and separately as a pamphlet. Six other books explaining the religious rather than the historical aspect of Quakerism are:

PENN, WILLIAM, *No Cross, No Crown* (obtainable from Friends Book Centre, London).
BRAYSHAW, A. NEAVE, *The Quakers: Their Story and Message.* Allen and Unwin, London, 4th ed., 1953.
BRINTON, HOWARD, *Friends for 300 Years.* Harper, New York 1952; Allen and Unwin, London.
(CERESOLE, PIERRE) *For Peace and Truth*, ed. by Harvey and Yates. Bannisdale, London, 1954
GRUBB, EDWARD, *What is Quakerism?* (numerous reprints, 1917–49). Allen and Unwin, London.
KELLY, THOMAS R., *A Testament of Devotion.* New York, 1941; Hodder and Stoughton, London, 1957